KNOWLEDGE MANAGEMENT FOR LIBRARIES

Library Technology Essentials

About the Series

The *Library Technology Essentials* series helps librarians utilize today's hottest new technologies as well as ready themselves for tomorrow's. The series features titles that cover the A–Z of how to leverage the latest and most cutting-edge technologies and trends to deliver new library services.

Today's forward-thinking libraries are responding to changes in information consumption, new technological advancements, and growing user expectations by devising groundbreaking ways to remain relevant in a rapidly changing digital world. This collection of primers guides libraries along the path to innovation through step-by-step instruction. Written by the field's top experts, these handbooks serve as the ultimate gateway to the newest and most promising emerging technology trends. Filled with practical advice and projects for libraries to implement right now, these books inspire readers to start leveraging these new techniques and tools today.

About the Series Editor

Ellyssa Kroski is the Director of Information Technology at the New York Law Institute as well as an award-winning editor and author of 22 books including *Law Librarianship in the Digital Age* for which she won the AALL's 2014 Joseph L. Andrews Legal Literature Award. Her ten-book technology series, The Tech Set, won the ALA's Best Book in Library Literature Award in 2011. She is a librarian, an adjunct faculty member at Pratt Institute, and an international conference speaker. She speaks at several conferences a year, mainly about new tech trends, digital strategy, and libraries.

Titles in the Series

1. *Wearable Technology: Smart Watches to Google Glass for Libraries*, by Tom Bruno
2. *MOOCs and Libraries*, by Kyle K. Courtney
3. *Free Technology for Libraries*, by Amy Deschenes
4. *Makerspaces in Libraries*, by Theresa Willingham and Jeroen De Boer
5. *Knowledge Management for Libraries*, by Valerie Forrestal
6. *WordPress for Libraries*, by Chad Haefele
7. *Game It Up!: Using Gamification to Incentivize Your Library*, by David Folmar
8. *Data Visualizations and Infographics*, by Sarah K. C. Mauldin
9. *Mobile Social Marketing in Libraries*, by Samantha C. Helmick
10. *Digital Collections and Exhibits*, by Juan Denzer
11. *Using Tablets and Apps in Libraries*, by Elizabeth Willse
12. *Responsive Web Design in Practice*, by Jason A. Clark

KNOWLEDGE MANAGEMENT FOR LIBRARIES

Valerie Forrestal

ROWMAN & LITTLEFIELD
Lanham • Boulder • New York • London

Published by Rowman & Littlefield
A wholly owned subsidary of The Rowman & Littlefield Publishing Group,
Inc.
4501 Forbes Boulevard, Suite 200, Lanham, Maryland 20706
www.rowman.com

Unit A, Whitacre Mews, 26-34 Stannary Street, London SE11 4AB

British Library Cataloguing in Publication Information Available

Library of Congress Cataloging-in-Publication Data

Forrestal, Valerie, 1978-
Knowledge management for libraries / Valerie Forrestal.
pages cm
Includes bibliographical references and index.
ISBN 978-1-4422-5302-5 (cloth : alk. paper) — ISBN 978-1-4422-5303-2 (pbk. : alk. paper) —
ISBN 978-1-4422-5304-9 (ebook)
1. Libraries—Information technology. 2. Knowledge management. 3. Libraries—Information re-
sources management. 4. Libraries—Communication systems. 5. Library information networks. 6.
Communication in library administration. I. Title.
Z678.9.F6487 2015
025.00285—dc23
2015011511

∞ ™ The paper used in this publication meets the minimum requirements of
American National Standard for Information Sciences Permanence of Paper
for Printed Library Materials, ANSI/NISO Z39.48-1992.

Printed in the United States of America

For my parents,
without whose support I could have
never found my calling

CONTENTS

SERIES EDITOR'S FOREWORD

Knowledge Management for Libraries is a one-stop manual for implementing a knowledge management system within your organization. This expertly written tome discusses harnessing the power of collaborative software for document management, communication and collaboration among remote team members, and creating valuable online reference tools. Readers will learn how to leverage the potential of today's best software to create internal knowledge bases and intranets within their organizations. Author Valerie Forrestal skillfully guides the reader through how to set up private staff social networks, construct document management systems, create an organizational commons, construct web-based knowledge bases, and even how to build a library intranet site using Microsoft SharePoint. Everything from planning to best practices can be found in this outstanding guide.

The idea for the Library Technology Essentials book series came about because there have been many drastic changes in information consumption, new technological advancements, and growing user expectations over the past few years which forward-thinking libraries are responding to by devising groundbreaking ways to remain relevant in a rapidly changing digital world. I saw a need for a practical set of guidebooks which libraries could use to inform themselves about how to stay on the cutting edge by implementing new programs, services, and technologies to match their patrons' expectations.

Libraries today are embracing new and emerging technologies, transforming themselves into community hubs and places of co-creation through makerspaces, developing information commons spaces, and even taking on new roles and formats, all the while searching for ways to decrease budget lines, add value, and prove the ROI (return on investment) of the library. The Library Technology Essentials series is a collection of primers to guide libraries along the path to innovation through step-by-step instruction. Written by the field's top experts, these handbooks are meant to serve as the ultimate gateway to the newest and most promising emerging technology trends. Filled with practical advice and project ideas for libraries to implement right now, these books will hopefully inspire readers to start leveraging these new techniques and tools today.

Each book follows the same format and outline, guiding the reader through the A–Z of how to leverage the latest and most cutting-edge technologies and trends to deliver new library services. Chapter 5 comprises the largest portion of the books, providing library initiatives that can be implemented by both beginner and advanced readers, accommodating for all audiences and levels of technical expertise. These projects and programs range from the basic—"How to Circulate Wearable Technology in Your Library" and "How to Host a FIRST Robotics Team at the Library"—to intermediate such as "How to Create a Hands-Free Digital Exhibit Showcase with Microsoft Kinect," to the more advanced options such as "Implementing a Scalable E-Resources Management System" and "How to Gamify Library Orientation for Patrons with a Top Down Video Game." Readers of all skill levels will find something of interest in these books.

Valerie Forrestal has been speaking and writing about emerging technology in libraries for many years, so I knew if anyone in the field would excel at writing a practical guide to leveraging collaborative software, it would be her. Her background as a web services librarian who designs and develops web-based systems and services lends itself very well to a handbook on knowledge management. If you're considering creating an intranet or launching a knowledge management initiative in your library and want guidance from an expert, you'll want to consult this book.

—Ellyssa Kroski
Director of Information Technology
The New York Law Institute
http://www.ellyssakroski.com

http://ccgclibraries.com
ellyssakroski@yahoo.com

PREFACE

Applying knowledge management (KM) techniques at your library can vastly improve efficiency and decision making by streamlining access to a department or organization's collected knowledge. KM systems allow you to leverage the potential of organizational knowledge in practical ways such as simplifying workflows and processes, and centralizing documentation.

The purpose of this guide is to serve as a practical introduction to the basic concept of knowledge management, and to familiarize you with a number of KM tools currently in use at institutions like your own, from the perspective of librarian and a technologist often tasked with selecting and deploying software to solve problems. Rather than reciting marketing jargon at the reader, this slender volume will show you how different KM tools are being used by professionals like yourself in the field of library and information science. It is my sincere hope that the case studies and projects outlined in this book will inspire you to implement or improve knowledge management practices at your own institution.

Chapter 1 is a basic introduction to the concept of knowledge management and the types of information that can be captured, stored, organized, and made accessible through knowledge base software. It also takes a look at why this is an important topic for libraries to consider, and how KM systems help add value to an organization.

Chapter 2 delves into the different purposes and types of knowledge bases available, and gives some planning and preparation tips to help you efficiently embark on a software-deployment project at your library.

Chapter 3 takes an in-depth look at specific programs, websites, and software solutions for building a knowledge base. It highlights the strengths of each service, focusing specifically on cost, time, effort, and level of skill required for setup. It also gives a fairly comprehensive overview of the various software commonly used for knowledge management in libraries and educational institutions.

Chapter 4 discusses some seminal case studies involving knowledge management system implementation in various libraries, focusing particularly on the software used in the projects chapter of the book. The case studies include insights shared by their authors about planning and managing similar implementation projects.

Chapter 5 outlines, step-by-step, how to build and launch a knowledge management system at your library, using a variety of software products, for a variety of purposes. Since different tools might work best for different purposes, you may want to take on more than one project over time, but each section of this chapter features a standalone project that will result in a working system all on its own.

Chapter 6 is a best practices chapter, which gives practical advice about planning, launching, and managing new technology in your library. This chapter takes its cue from the field of project management, but also shares a healthy dose of "learning from other people's mistakes." Don't worry, no names will be named.

Chapter 7 looks down the road a bit into the future of knowledge management systems in educational settings. Thinking about future functionality and needs may well affect the decisions you make about what technology you invest in today.

Finally, chapter 8 is a list of recommended reading, broken down into "Articles" and "Case Studies" (including all the case studies mentioned in chapter 4), "Books," and "Online Documentation and Help Guides." The "Books" and "Online Documentation" sections will be particularly useful for those who are looking for more information about the software discussed in the book, for troubleshooting, or for going beyond the scope of the projects outlined in this book.

ACKNOWLEDGMENTS

There are so many people (and cats) without whom this book would not have been possible. First and foremost of those is Ellyssa Kroski, the series editor, who was kind enough to include me in this endeavor. I truly hope I have not let her down.

I've said this already, but I'll say it again: thank you to my family for supporting me through all my various educational and career choices. Librarianship is truly my calling in life, and I couldn't have found my way here if they hadn't helped me out financially and emotionally through the years. A special thank you to my brother, who let me use his lovely home as a writer's retreat. I'm sorry about that time I broke your hot tub.

I'd also like to thank the ladies of my cabal, specifically Kristi Chadwick, Carolyn Ciesla, Anne Heidemann, Sarah Jones, Julie Jurgens, Anna Mickelsen, Beth Nerbonne, Lisa Rabey, Amanda Roberts, Sarah Strahl, and of course my soul sister, partner in crime, and fellow ghost rights advocate and paranormal real estate agent, Kristin LaLonde. (SKEPTIC! DRINK!) You ladies inspire me, make me think, make me laugh, and give the most amazing hugs. I am so honored and thankful to have you in my life.

Thank you also to the fabulous Heidi Page, who helped take my mind off work with wine and crafting. We've been BFFs since we met at a pep rally freshman year of high school (you had me at "hell, no"). You're amazing, I love you, and I wouldn't let you out of my life if you tried, so don't bother trying.

Sincerest thanks to my colleague, mentor, and dear friend, Barbara Arnett. Without your encouragement and help I would've never had the ambition or the nerve to turn my dabbling in technology into a career move. You're a genius, and together we are an unstoppable force of nature. Or rather we would be if not for happy hour. I look forward to our inevitable retirement to the country, where we will drink much wine, amass an army of cats, and probably build a time machine (or at least engage in some really cool steampunk cosplay).

A special shout out to my colleague Brian Farr, without whose constant prodding and daily coffee runs I definitely wouldn't have made it past page 10 of this book. You're tough, but fair, my friend.

I am eternally grateful to the wonderful, encouraging, snarky, brilliant, and innovative community of librarians that I belong to, both online and locally. I'm incredibly humbled and thankful for all the support you've provided me with over the years, especially while working on this book. I don't know many other professional communities that are as competitive and yet as simultaneously supportive as librarians. You challenge me and push me to grow, but are never stingy with the high fives. I'd send each and every one of you a tiara if I could. (I'm working on it.)

Finally, last but *definitely* not least, I'd like to thank my kitties, Nibbler T. Noms, Ike E. Puppy, Oliver P. Puppycat, Carmine Martin McDonald Roger Benedict (aka Benny), and my dear, departed Kiku. Without your purrs and snuggles I don't know what the point of anything would be.

AN INTRODUCTION TO KNOWLEDGE MANAGEMENT

An Introduction to Knowledge Management

As librarians we've become expert information managers. We've learned to sort, filter, organize, and facilitate access to information through many platforms and on many levels. In the time- and resource-crunched world of libraries, we rightly focus our attention on our users, and the issues and concerns that arise in the back office can get lost in the mix.

Books, journals, and technology are key components of any modern library, but a library's most valuable asset is its staff. Providing platforms that can capture the knowledge and expertise of your staff, and facilitate communication and professional development among them, is an investment that will only build in value over the years. Also, often talked about in the profession is the gap between the theoretical knowledge which students gain in MLIS (master of library and information science) programs, and the practical knowledge that can only be accrued from years on the job. However, it's often hard to bridge that gap in the workplace, where fresh ideas and solid experience should mingle on a regular basis to fuel both innovation and competence.

This book will show you how to implement tools which will help your colleagues communicate, collaborate, share documents and files, and greatly clarify and simplify workflows. You'll likely find that one or two of the tools outlined meet your needs, so don't be overwhelmed by the number of projects included in the book. Think of them as options, and find the one(s) that best suit your library's needs. You may also want to give some thought to whether you'd like to implement a few quick and easy projects, or embark on one of the more involved projects which could solve more of your problems with one tool. There's no right answer, so take the time to decide what's right for you and your library!

The software solutions discussed in the coming chapters can be set up and administered with a minimum of technical expertise, but proper planning and thoughtful implementation are important, so the strengths of each tool will be discussed, as well as the tips and strategies for getting the most out of them. Most of the software mentioned in this book is free and mostly cloud-based, so you don't need your own server space to set it up. When this is not the case, options and resources for making it work will be provided.

Mostly, this book (all the books in this series, in fact!) aims to inspire you to try out new technology in your library, whether it's for yourself, your department, an event or group you're involved in, or your whole library. Some projects have been outlined for you, step-by-step, with enough information to get you well on your way without overwhelming you with every single feature or function the highlighted software has available. This book also makes a concerted effort to provide extra clarification for any tricky areas where users commonly get stuck or confused, and gives you a heads-up for what to look out for. At the end of the book there is a suggested reading list which will provide more in-depth information if you get really stuck or want to delve deeper.

WHAT IS KNOWLEDGE MANAGEMENT?

Knowledge management (KM) is a concept that came out of the organizational management field in the mid-1990s. The idea was formally born in academia, but caught on like wildfire in the business world soon after. The thinking was that the value of an organization lies not just in its physical assets and the services it provides, but also in the collective know-how of its employees. This collective knowledge, talent, and experience of an organization's staff became known as intellectual capital. Managers and investors quickly realized that intellectual capital was not just an indicator of an organization's ability to succeed in the present, but also how it will adapt and grow in the future.

What intellectual capital really boils down to is people power. No matter how impressive the current state of computing, the human brain remains the best tool for learning, adapting, and using past experience and understanding to respond creatively to new problems and challenges. Proponents of KM theory know that knowledge is connected, and that you can tap into your organization's people power to add value to information and to facilitate connections that otherwise never would have been made.

And so the business world set out to capitalize on this new concept of knowledge management by building tools to leverage the intellectual capital of an organization. There are many kinds of KM platforms, including e-learning systems, data mining and analysis programs, resource portals, and content management systems. This book talks mainly about portals and content management systems, which in the context of this topic are referred to collectively as knowledge bases.

WHAT IS A KNOWLEDGE BASE?

In KM, a knowledge base is the software or platform used to collect, organize, and facilitate access to information (usually generated by your employees). Unlike knowledge bases in the field of computer science, which are built to be mainly automated and machine-readable, KM knowledge bases are designed to be used by humans, meaning they have an interface which guides users through the process of adding and retrieving information. In fact, a good knowledge base does not just act as a repository of information, documents, and files, but adds functionality to help users organize and put that information in context, by connecting it to related information or resources, so that organizational knowledge exists as a part of a connected whole and not just as isolated pieces of data.

Logistically, the goal of a knowledge base is to capture knowledge from all parts of an organization, and to remove barriers between the person or department in which the knowledge is held, and the person or people who need it. This is especially important for workplaces where staff may have disparate schedules (for example when there are many part-time employees with different shifts), or workplaces that have or will soon have new or retiring staff members. Knowledge bases enable you to transfer knowledge across shifts and from departing employees to new hires, and allow you to create an ever-evolving resource which capitalizes both on fresh insight and seasoned experience.

Knowledge bases can deal with both explicit (easily articulated) and tacit (personal, difficult to communicate) knowledge. By supporting features like tagging, categories, image and multimedia embedding, and natural-language searching, systems can build meaning around information that had before been hard to describe or quantify. And where tacit knowledge cannot be made explicit, social features can help directly connect you with the person who holds that knowledge.

WHY IS KNOWLEDGE MANAGEMENT IMPORTANT IN LIBRARIES?

Libraries are in the business of information. Libraries are also in the customer service business. As librarians, we want to help our patrons achieve whatever task they set out to accomplish when they came to the library, and we want to do it as thoroughly and efficiently as possible. Having tools at the ready which allow librarians to pool common knowledge and access it at a moment's notice keeps us from wasting the patron's time searching across resources, or tracking down a specific person who might have the answer or the knowledge being sought. (Tight budgets have always made it necessary for librarians to be masters of multitasking, after all.)

You may have also heard rumors of an imminent mass-retirement in the library profession. As someone who first heard those rumors many years ago, I am certainly not ringing any alarm bells about the prospect. But I have worked in environments where a vital staff member retired without leaving much documentation about their job functions, so I can attest to the importance of capturing and sharing staff knowledge before it's too late. And especially in today's digital world, information about account numbers, usernames, and passwords become vital documentation to have on-hand.

As mentioned earlier, obviously not all organizational knowledge can be captured and catalogued in a knowledge base. Subject specialists and domain experts are, and will remain, vital to the profession, but knowledge bases free up everyone's time just a little, so librarians can focus on research, in-depth reference, teaching, collection development, and other important job duties, thus showcasing our true value as information professionals.

2

GETTING STARTED WITH KNOWLEDGE MANAGEMENT

Getting Started with Knowledge Management

Regardless of your budget or your technical know-how, there are tools to help you implement some basic knowledge management (KM) practices at your library, in no time at all! These KM tools can solve many communication and information-sharing problems, but before embarking on any of the projects in this book, it's helpful to understand knowledge bases in their broader sense, and to think about your library's individual needs, workflows, and technology infrastructure.

TYPES OF KNOWLEDGE BASES

Knowledge bases can serve a wide variety of purposes, but the four main reasons most organizations implement this type of software are

1. to facilitate, enhance, and archive communication;
2. to create a repository for documents, files, forms, and other ephemera (usually one with features which support collaboration in some form);
3. to organize information, document common workflows or processes, and/or list common questions and their answers; and

4. to provide a single portal to multiple resources, documents, tools, and applications used by staff.

Most types of knowledge base software can actually do all four tasks to some extent, but all tools tend to excel at one or two of these things at the expense of the others, so it makes sense to think about your organization's needs and priorities before deciding on what projects to embark upon.

Knowledge base software can be hosted locally, meaning it is installed on your organization's own servers, or it can be cloud-based, meaning it resides on the remote servers of the company who makes the software, or remote shared servers. Usually locally hosted options offer greater customization options, but also may require a bit more technical expertise. *Note*: If you don't have access to your organization's server space, you can also use a hosting company like Amazon Web Services or Bluehost.

CHOOSING THE RIGHT TOOL FOR THE JOB

One of the first things you should think about before embarking on any sort of technology implementation project is scalability. You may want to start a knowledge base for just one department in your library, but if it is a successful and popular tool, can it be expanded to be used by the whole library? If you decide to use it to collect and share information about an event or a committee, can it easily be used for future events or committees without overwriting the previous content?

All of the software we will discuss in the "Projects" chapter of this book can easily be started as a smaller project, and then expanded if necessary. Google Drive allows you to create folders with different permissions, so you can create a folder for each department and/or working group, and staff will only have access to the ones specifically shared with them. WordPress Commons allows users to create groups, which can be open or private, so you can set up as many online spaces with custom user groups as you need for your library. Microsoft SharePoint lets you create sites with their own customizations and permissions for each department or group. These features will be discussed more indepth later in this book, but it will help to keep in mind while in the planning stages how you would expand your knowledge base if you later decide that you need to.

Chapter 3 will go over each of the tools used in the projects section of this book, and will look at them from the following angles:

- cost;
- skill level;
- effort;
- scalability; and
- strengths.

The strengths (and weaknesses) of each tool are relative to your desired purpose for launching the software. As mentioned earlier, these purposes are generally communicating, storing documents, organizing information, and streamlining access to multiple resources (i.e., a portal). You should think about these issues and their importance when taking on any project. Projects that can work well in tandem will also be highlighted, since some tools can complement each other and work really well together, as opposed to trying to force software into doing something it's not so great at.

PLANNING

Before implementing any new software in your library, there are some simple steps you can take to help push the project toward success. Spend a little time talking to staff members who will use the software. What is their current workflow like? What problems do they encounter on a daily basis? These questions are important because they are the key to creating excitement and getting buy-in for your project.

The further away from their current workflow the new tool is, the more training that will be necessary. For example, if they are used to coming into work and signing into an online system, like a web-based e-mail portal or intranet, then replacing that sign-in process with a different one may not be a big deal. Adding another thing to sign into will make them less likely to remember unless you provide incentives or reminders. Changing their workflow all together will be more difficult. If they are used to getting documentation from a book which sits at the reference desk, it may take some time for them to get used to looking online for that information. In this case, it will help to create an easily findable shortcut on shared computers, and, after fair warning, you may need to remove the physical copies.

Paying attention to problems the staff is encountering in their daily job duties can also be very helpful in implementing new technology. They may be reluctant to change their current way of doing things, but if the new way makes their lives easier, they will be more likely to give it a try. Also, while you're asking questions and assessing workflow, it's also helpful to find employees who are willing to be beta testers or early adopters of the new system. These staff members will be an invaluable resource, not only in providing feedback which you can use to improve the system, but also as advocates and trainers who can help get other staff members excited about the project, and provide extra help on the fly to those who need it.

Another crucial step in the planning process is to identify and locate the content you will want to migrate into your new online system. This could include physical content (like paper manuals and forms, which will need to later be scanned or retyped), digital content that is spread out across various computers and servers (like meeting minutes and reports), and also ephemeral content like important links, resources, and tacit knowledge from staff (which will need to be collected and entered into the system). When building a knowledge base, it's important to pre-populate the system with content before launch, so staff can experiment with it and get a good sense of its purpose and usefulness. Having this content ready for population into the system early in the process will save you a headache later.

Finally, think about best practices. This book will discuss best practices often, but you or your organization may have specific rules or preferences that must be followed or workflows that differ from other libraries. Whatever software you decide to use, look around the Internet for other libraries that have implemented it, or ask around in your social and personal learning networks. Make a note of what you like about their implementations, and what you don't. What works for another library may not work for your library, so it's okay to take a look with a critical eye! Sometimes knowing what you *don't* want is just as important as knowing what you want.

3

TOOLS AND APPLICATIONS

Let's dive into some of the tools which will be used for the projects outlined in this book, and also some other useful websites and software that you may want to check out. Chapter 5 will take a much closer look at individual functions and features, but this overview will help you understand the capabilities and strengths of each application, so you can have a better idea of which projects you'd like to experiment with at your library, or even at home!

GOOGLE DRIVE

Google Drive is a cloud-based file storage and document collaboration tool. You can upload word processing files, presentations, spreadsheets, images, and PDFs, or you can create documents in Google's own format, which displays pretty much the same way as regular documents from Microsoft or Adobe. *Note*: A free account gives you 15 GB of online storage space for files, but documents saved as Google Docs, Sheets, or Slides do not count towards your storage limit. You can also purchase an extra 100 GB of space for $1.99 per month.

Many people use Google Drive simply to have access to their files from anywhere they can log into their Google account. I often recommend to patrons that they use Google Drive instead of a flash drive, since they are always forgetting their flash drives in the computers and losing them! But Google Drive can be used for more than just storing and syncing files across devices. You can also use it to create forms, share documents with others so they can edit or comment on them, or to create a public URL for a document or flyer so it can be shared via social media or e-mail.

Google Drive is also great for collaborating on documents because it allows you to control what kind of access you give your collaborators, and lets you track edits and activity by them. You can set various permission levels when sharing a document so that other users can only view it, make comments on it, or make edits. You can also view older versions of a document and roll back changes that have been made by restoring a previous version. Also, when you log into Google Drive, the activity panel shows recent edits and uploads, so you can see who has been working on what files in the system.

The last chapter mentioned some metrics for assessing each of the tools discussed in chapter 5, so table 3.1 gives a quick run-down of Google Drive's key stats, functions, and assets.

Table 3.1.   Google Drive

Website:	• http://drive.google.com
Cost:	• Free for the first 15 GB • $1.99/month for extra storage
Skill level:	• No special technical skills required beyond basic Internet and word processing ability
Effort:	• Easy as creating a Google account • Upload or create a new file or folder in 2 clicks • Files and folders are drag and drop for easy organizing
Scalability:	• Only the first 15 GB is free, but under $25/year for 100 GB is still quite reasonable and plenty of storage for most file types (audio and video files take up a lot of space) • The folder system allows you to create any number of subfolders, much like on a personal computer, so you can easily expand and organize a large number of files
Strengths:	• File storage, organization, and access • Document sharing and collaboration • Data collection and aggregation
Notable Features:	• Activity tracking for files and folders • Adjustable permission levels to control access to folders and files • Advanced/full-text file search and sort functions • Chat function for co-collaborators • Cross-device syncing • File versioning • Offline access • Optical character recognition (OCR) for images and PDFs

PBWORKS

PBworks is a website that allows you to easily create a public or private wiki. A wiki is just an application that lets you build simple websites which are usually used for content management, information organization, and online collaboration. PBworks is a cloud-based tool, so you don't have to install any software on your server or your computer; you can access and edit your wiki through any web browser.

The PBworks website offers different free options depending on the scope of your project. The versions most commonly used by libraries and educational institutions are their EDUHub and WIKIHub products. While the software is the same for all free versions of PBworks, EDUHub offers unlimited user accounts and more storage for free, but restricts you to one wiki, while WIKIHub allows for only fifteen users, but you can create up to five individual wikis (see figure 3.1).

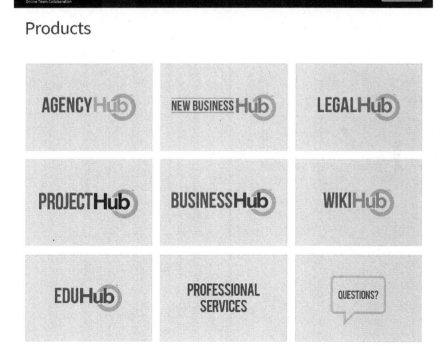

Figure 3.1.   PBworks products and services

PBworks wikis are great for collaborating with colleagues on creating documentation, such as policies, procedures, or help guides (see table 3.2). They also work well for collecting and sharing information about an event, project, or committee. You can make your wiki public on the web, or you can restrict access to specific users, who can be assigned various permissions from just being able to view the wiki (or specific pages within it), to being able to edit the wiki (or specific pages), to having full access to pages and settings.

You can edit the content of wiki pages through a word-processor styled interface in PBworks, which also allows you to add links, images, and media. There is also a tab on the site which allows you to view a list of all the pages and folders you've created, as well as any files you've uploaded. The list is drag-and-drop so it is easy to move items into folders to organize your content.

PBworks wikis also feature a sidebar which is visible on every page and can be used to create persistent navigation for the wiki, or any other list of links or important information that you want users to have easy access to. Under the sidebar is an activity pane, similar to the one discussed in the Google Drive section. This pane allows you to see who has created, moved, or edited files in the recent past. Also similar to Google Drive, PBworks wiki pages each have a revision history, which allows you to view, compare, and revert back to various past versions of the page.

Table 3.2.   PBworks

Website:	• http://pbworks.com
Cost:	• Free for 1 wiki + 2 GB of storage + 100 users on EDUHub • Free for 5 wikis + 50 MB of storage + 15 users on WIKIHub • $99–$1995/year for extra storage/users/features/customizations
Skill level:	• No special technical skills required beyond basic Internet and word processing ability • Some familiarity with basic HTML is helpful, but not required
Effort:	• Create a new wiki in five clicks • Word-processor-like text editing • Drag and drop pages and folders for easy organizing • Majority of effort is in planning, content creation/migration, and organizing content
Scalability:	• Free accounts are limited in scope and good for either one large project or a small organization

- Wikis cannot be switched from one type of account to another, so you cannot move an EDUHub wiki to WIKIHub if the scope or focus of the wiki later changes
- Although EDUHub only allows each user to create one wiki, there is no hard limit on number of users or number of pages
- Self-created navigation and drag and drop pages and folders make reorganization a fairly easy process

Strengths:	• Content management and collaboration • Information organization • File storage
Notable Features:	• Activity tracking pane • Adjustable permission levels to control access to pages • Customizable sidebar area • Embeddable media and plugins • HTML export for pages (does not include uploaded files) • One-click create/upload/share functions • Optional page commenting • Page versioning • RSS support • Word-processor-like interface for editing page content

YAMMER

Knowledge is a social enterprise these days, so having your own organizational social network is a great way to tap into social energy and harness it to create a knowledge base. Microsoft's Yammer lets you easily create an internal social network that looks and acts a lot like Facebook, but without the ads or the distractions. On Yammer, you have the ability to create a profile, upload files, post announcements, and exchange messages with other users (see table 3.3). There is also a chat function, a built-in survey tool, and an apps directory full of useful productivity applications for goal-tracking, brainstorming, training, and collaboration. There are even games to help you get to know your colleagues, or to celebrate achievements with digital badges.

Yammer specializes in helping users make meaningful connections by suggesting relevant groups or colleagues with similar interests or specialties. Users can choose to add their contact information, work and educational background, and/or relevant links to their profile to help colleagues find and connect with each other. The social-style activity feed aggregates network and group activity into streams, which can be customized by users. To help organize content, and to allow you to keep up with updates that are important to you, users can tag content by topic, and those topics can be added or removed from your content stream. Important posts, announcements, or events can also be shared or bookmarked individually. For users who may not log into their Yammer network every day, you can set up e-mail notifications for certain kinds of activity within your network or groups.

But Yammer is not only a social network. You can upload and collaborate on documents, tag and link related files, discuss edits, or ask questions in a document's feed. Yammer's advanced commenting functionality lets users highlight, cross out text, add comments, and even write freehand on an uploaded file. Yammer also maintains a revision history for files, which allows you to view and, if necessary, revert back to previous versions of the document.

Table 3.3.   Yammer

Website:	• http://yammer.com
Cost:	• Free for Yammer Basic Edition • $3/month per user for Yammer Enterprise Edition • Yammer Enterprise is free with Office 365 Enterprise or Education
Skill level:	• Familiarity with websites with social features is helpful • Comfort with adding/using plug-ins/widgets/add-ons for websites
Effort:	• As easy as setting up a Facebook account for yourself. • Social functions are familiar and intuitive • Invite new users or install apps to the network in two clicks
Scalability:	• Ability to create groups allows you to have one organizational network and expand it to departments, projects, or committees • Can be integrated with other Microsoft products like Office 365 and SharePoint Intranet • Functionality can be expanded and customized with over eighty available add-on applications
Strengths:	• Communication • Collaboration • Portal
Notable Features:	• Document collaboration • Instant messaging • Mobile apps for Android, iPhone, iPad, and Windows Phones • Network, group, and document activity feeds • Over eighty apps to customize and add features to your network • Simple built-in polling tool • Topic tagging for organizing content

WORDPRESS + CBOX

WordPress is an online platform that can be used for many purposes from blogging, to content management, to social networking (see table 3.4). WordPress can be hosted on a local server, hosted with a web-hosting company like Amazon Web Services, Bluehost, HostGator, or WPEngine, or can be cloud-hosted through WordPress.com.

A team at the City University of New York (CUNY) has also put together a suite of tools to create an online organizational commons. An online commons is just a shared web space for people to communicate and interact. CUNY's Commons in a Box (CBOX) project allows you to easily install a pre-packaged set of plug-ins to turn any WordPress installation into an instant online community, with user accounts and profiles, private and public groups, unlimited blogs, built-in wiki software, document storage and collaboration, discussion forums, and private messaging.

Table 3.4. WordPress

Website:	• http://wordpress.org (to download the WordPress software) • commonsinabox.org (to download the CBOX WordPress plugin)
Cost:	• Free (though if you don't have your own server space it will cost about $25/month to set up WordPress through a web-hosting company.)
Skill level:	• Some technical expertise is necessary for configuring server and database settings • Familiarity with the WordPress environment is helpful, but not necessary
Effort:	• Easy software installation • Plug-ins require additional setup and customization • Most of the time and effort is in the setup, then users take control of creating and moderating groups and discussions • Occasional software updates required • Simple group and blog setup with just a few clicks
Scalability:	• Network scales easily with no hard limit on the number of users, groups, blogs, wiki pages, or uploads
Strengths:	• Communication • Document Sharing and Collaboration
Notable Features:	• Built-in wiki • Customizable activity streams • Document upload and collaboration with BuddyPress Docs • Image slider/carousel for news and announcements • User-created blogs and groups

MICROSOFT SHAREPOINT

Microsoft SharePoint is a comprehensive intranet solution which allows you to build sites for your organization, departments, groups, committees, and so forth (see table 3.5). The software can be installed on your own server (some Windows servers even come with a basic version of SharePoint preinstalled) or you can subscribe to their cloud-hosted version, SharePoint Online. Either version allows you to easily build sites that give your users access to important links, documents, calendars, resources, and collaboration and communication tools.

You can think of each site as a portal to all the important tools people need to do their jobs. SharePoint even offers apps that you can embed in your site's pages to add functionality like document collaboration, shared calendars, and task management. SharePoint also offers a wide variety of security and permission options, so you can restrict access to various sites, apps, and documents, as necessary.

Table 3.5.   Microsoft SharePoint

Website:	• http://products.office.com/sharepoint
Cost:	• Free for SharePoint Server Standard Edition • $5/user/month for SharePoint Online • (You may also be eligible for a free site/sites if your organization already has a SharePoint or Office 365 license.)
Skill level:	• Some technical expertise required if installing software on local server • Familiarity with web content management systems is helpful, but not required
Effort:	• Successful implementation does require a decent amount of effort in the planning and launch stages (i.e., requirements-gathering, user testing, and training) • Creating sites and adding apps is quick and easy, but customization and configuration can take some time
Scalability:	• Network scales easily with additional team sites and/or subsites, and a multitude of available apps to add functionality • Permissions are inherited from their parent site, so they can be tricky. Pay particular attention to this section of the projects chapter in this book.
Strengths:	• Document sharing and collaboration • Content management • Communication • Portal
Notable Features:	• Adjustable permission levels to control access to sites, libraries, and files • Available version control for document libraries

- Built-in wiki
- Customizable homepage for each site/subsite
- Document upload and collaboration
- Embeddable media and plugins
- Mobile apps for Android, iPhone, iPad, and Windows Phones
- Over six hundred apps to customize and add features to your network
- Seamless Microsoft Office and Yammer integration

LIBANSWERS

LibAnswers is a cloud-based software product from Springshare which allows libraries to build comprehensive question-and-answer style knowledge bases (see table 3.6). The system can be used both as publicly available "Frequently Asked Questions" (FAQ) tool, and as an internal repository for policies and other commonly asked reference questions. LibAnswers modules can be customized and embedded in other website or pages, and the software is optimized for viewing on any size monitor or device. You can also add images, multimedia, attached files, related resources, and topic categories to answers to help enhance your content and make information easier for users to find.

Users can search the knowledge base by keyword, topic, or question, or they can submit their own question if they can't find the information they need within the system. Questions can be submitted through e-mail (you choose what e-mail addresses get imported into the system), through the included chat module via customizable widgets which you can embed in other websites or pages, and also through your library's Twitter account, which can be linked within LibAnswers. You can also create queues for different departments or librarians, and questions can be routed by department or subject area.

LibAnswers allows you to build your knowledge base by manually adding content, and also by adding questions entered into the system via your LibAnswers website, LibAnswers widgets, email, chat, SMS/text message or Twitter. You can also track and generate reports on questions submitted to the system, keywords being searched, and number of question and topic views through the reference analytics module.

Table 3.6.   LibAnswers

Website:	• http://springshare.com/libanswers
Cost:	• $599/year to $1099/year depending on size of library (FTE or # of card-holders) • $299/year to $699/year for optional analytics module
Skill level:	• Some HTML experience is helpful for customizing site design and creating and integrating widgets in other sites/pages • Familiarity with form-creation software or websites is helpful (Microsoft Access, SurveyMonkey, or Google Forms, for example)
Effort:	• Content is easily migrated from other sources via a word-processor-like interface • Easily add user-submitted questions to the public knowledge base • In order to create practical and useful analytics reports, some thought needs to be given to assigning meaningful metadata categories to questions
Scalability:	• Create unlimited FAQ/knowledge bases for different departments or user groups • Question queues allow you to easily add multiple departments and route questions appropriately • As content grows, FAQ(s) can be organized through groups and/or topic tags
Strengths:	• FAQ • Collaborative content management and information organization • Portal • Data collection and aggregation
Notable Features:	• Auto-complete search form helps guide users to relevant topics • Customizable, embeddable widgets • Free domain-mapping so you can use your institution's URL without hosting any software • Integrated chat and SMS reference tools at no extra cost • Mobile and tablet-friendly design • QuerySpy tool allows you to view keywords being searched in real-time, even if the user never submits a question

OTHER KNOWLEDGE MANAGEMENT TOOLS

Alternative Tools for Document Management

- Dropbox: https://www.dropbox.com
- Microsoft OneDrive: https://onedrive.live.com

Google Drive is obviously not the only game in town when it comes to storing and organizing documents in the cloud. Two other popular alternatives are Dropbox and OneDrive from Microsoft. Dropbox is extremely popular as a tool for temporary online storage of files. For example, if you are teaching a class or giving a presentation, you can upload your materials so that they will be available from any device with an Internet connection, which is a great alternative to (or back up for) storing those resources on a USB flash drive. Dropbox is also great for creating shared folders which entire groups or classes can upload to, so you can have group or class members submit projects or documents to the folder for easy access and collaboration.

For personal uses, Dropbox is free for up to 2 GB of storage, with the ability to earn additional free storage by successfully referring new users. You can get up to a terabyte (1,000 GB) of storage for $9.99 per month. There is also a business version of Dropbox that gives your organization additional features and unlimited storage for $15 a month per user.

Dropbox has a basic versioning system, where you can view older saved versions of the same file. It does not, however, give you an option to add your own metadata (or to even tag your files with keywords), so it might not be the best tool for permanently storing a large number of files with a complicated organization scheme. Dropbox has both mobile and desktop apps to allow you to access and sync your files across devices.

Microsoft's OneDrive (formerly called SkyDrive) features a very similar pricing scheme to Google Drive: 15 GB for free, 100 GB for $1.99 per month, and $6.99 for 1 TB. OneDrive is particularly useful for those operating in a mainly Microsoft environment, as it integrates seamlessly with Office products, and even mounts as its own drive in Windows 8+. There are also a multitude of writing, productivity, and collaboration apps which work with OneDrive, including apps for Easy-Bib and OneNote.

ALTERNATIVE WIKI ENGINE SOFTWARE

- MediaWiki: https://www.mediawiki.org/wiki/MediaWiki
- Wikispaces: https://www.wikispaces.com/

PBworks was chosen for the wiki project in this book because it is easy to use, cloud-based, and has a free option which will work for most libraries. There are many options, though, when looking at wiki software, including MediaWiki, the software used to build Wikipedia, and Wikispaces, another wiki platform which is popular in educational settings.

MediaWiki is free, open-source software that you install on your own server. This makes it a good option if you're looking to host your wiki locally, but it also means it should be installed and maintained by someone with a little bit of technical expertise, like a systems administrator or systems librarian. The software is written in PHP (hypertext preprocessor), which is a very common coding language (WordPress is also written in PHP), so it can be customized. Because MediaWiki is best suited for larger projects with content that is openly available, there is also a free enterprise version of MediaWiki called BlueSpice (http://www.blue-spice.org) which adds functionality, is a bit more user-friendly, and has better security options for restricting access to wiki pages.

Similar to PBworks, Wikispaces is cloud-based and offers a free version for educators. Although it is aimed at classroom use, with features to support assignments and assessment, it can easily be used for information and content management in most organizations. Wikispaces also has social features like discussion boards and activity feeds, and is built to integrate with other learning management tools such as Moodle, Blackboard, and Sakai. If you need more storage space, more customization options, or a greater number of users, there are paid plans for $200 per year for 5 GB of storage, and $1,000 per year for unlimited storage and 100 users.

Alternative Social Network or Online Commons Platforms

- BuddyPress (WordPress): https://buddypress.org/
- Ning: http://www.ning.com/
- SocialGO: http://www.socialgo.com/
- SocialEngine: http://www.socialengine.com/
- PHPfox: http://moxi9.com/phpfox

Chapter 5 discusses building a private social network for your organization with Yammer, and building an organizational commons with the

Commons in a Box (CBOX) plugin for WordPress. You might be wondering what the difference is between a "social network" and an "online commons," and the truth is that the terms could possibly be used interchangeably, but individually they represent a difference in focus. Though they both support communication and group/project work, Yammer focuses on productivity and interaction, while CBOX is built around a blogging platform, so users have more freedom to develop a personal space for expression and self-publishing.

The overarching motivation behind launching an online community for your organization is to help staff members to communicate and collaborate better. A large part of this is giving each user their own space to list important details about themselves, like education and professional experience, activities, and affiliations. The network must also have a way to search these profiles, so people can find each other to work on specialized projects or committees, and a variety of ways for users to then communicate with each other, as well as the ability to create spaces to collaborate on those projects and committees.

BuddyPress is a plugin which instantly turns WordPress into a social networking platform, and is actually one of the key components of the suite of tools included in the CBOX plugin. Adding BuddyPress to a WordPress installation adds features like user profiles, activity streams, user groups, user blogs, discussion forums, friend connections, collaborative work spaces, and private messaging. The confusing part about BuddyPress, however, is that while it is itself a WordPress plugin, once installed, it has its own list of over five hundred additional plugins, so knowing which set gives you the exact functionality you need while all working well together can be confusing. This is why chapter 5 deals specifically with CBOX, rather than just basic BuddyPress. But if you are very familiar with WordPress, and have a very specific set of needs for your online network, you may want to just use plain old BuddyPress instead. This will give you more room for customization, but will also take up a bit more time to set up and maintain the site.

In the past, Ning was the go-to website for creating custom social networks for your organization, group, or special interests. In fact, the Library 2.0 network on Ning (http://www.library20.com/) has been a very popular place for librarians to network online (though its focus has changed in recent years and it is now mostly conference-based). Although Ning is no longer a free web service, it is still a popular option for groups that are looking for a ready-made online community without the worry of installing any software or finding a remote hosting provider. For just $25 a month, you get up to 1,000 users, social tools like forums, activity feeds, photo sharing and liking, groups, profiles, and integration with other websites for cross-network sign-in and sharing. Ning also features blogging capability, responsive design for optimal viewing on any device, and easy, drag-and-drop site design.

SocialGO is another custom social network web service, with many similar features to Ning. SocialGO offers a $9.99 per month option for their basic service with unlimited users, or a premium package for $29.99 per month which adds customization options, more storage, and an audio/video chat function, which is an excellent tool for libraries with multiple branches, staff working different shifts, or work-from-home colleagues. SocialGO also promises to make your content available to you for download, should you ever decide to leave the service.

Two popular options for self-hosted social networks (besides WordPress-based software) are SocialEngine and PHPfox. Both offer one-time fee licensing (both starting at $299) and are fully customizable, with all the same social features as Ning or SocialGO. Similar to WordPress, both platforms have available themes and add-ons to customize and add functionality to your site, so while knowledge of PHP, HTML, and/or CSS is helpful, it is not necessary to build and launch a custom network. SocialEngine also offers a cloud-based version of the software as a subscription service for $29.99 per month.

Alternative Intranet Software

- Open Atrium (Drupal): http://www.openatrium.com/ https://www.drupal.org/project/openatrium
- Sakai: https://sakaiproject.org/

As for intranet software, chapter 5 includes a clear, step-by-step guide to setting up your library intranet with Microsoft SharePoint, because many organizations are already using the software, and can be overwhelmed by the options and capabilities. SharePoint can do so many things that sometimes even the reference and help documentation for the software can be a bit confusing, so the project guides you through the process of setting up a basic portal with some web parts with the specific needs of libraries in mind.

If you'd rather not use proprietary software and you're feeling a bit adventurous, and if you have some server space (either locally or hosted), you can try installing an open source intranet platform like Open Atrium or Sakai. Open Atrium is based on the open source content management system Drupal, and features modules for document storage and collaboration, project and event management, file and multimedia storage and embeds, communication and discussion, subsite and wiki creation, security, permissions, and authentication, and issue tracking, along with a variety of social tools. After you've downloaded the software, Open Atrium has a simple web-based install script, and can be installed with one click with certain hosting companies like Pantheon (https://www.getpantheon.com/). Once installed, you simply drag and drop elements into your dashboards and landing pages to design your site.

Sakai is actually an open source learning management system that was developed by several universities in the United States, but it can also work extremely well as an intranet platform, with tools for communication, collaboration, file sharing, scheduling, and general content management. Like Open Atrium, Sakai is free software that must be installed locally, or through a hosting company. The Sakai website lists some recommended hosting companies who also offer (fee-based) support for the software should you encounter problems. On the Sakai website you will also find pre-built demo sites for download, so you can easily try the software out before choosing it for full-scale implementation at your organization.

Alternative FAQ-Building Tools

- LibStats: https://code.google.com/p/libstats/
- Question2Answer (http://www.question2answer.org/)
- SubjectsPlus

When it comes to building a traditional knowledge base, many people think of FAQ documents. These tools present information in the popular question-and-answer format, because most information-seeking scenarios begin with a specific question, like "how do I go about doing this task?" or "where is this information or item located?" This book looks in-depth at setting up the FAQ tool LibAnswers because it was created by Springshare, and integrates with their other popular library products like LibGuides and LibChat, but it is by no means the only option for building library FAQ websites.

If you're looking for a free FAQ tool and you have server space available either locally or through a hosting company, there are some open source software options, including LibStats, Question2Answer, and SubjectsPlus. Question2Answer is the only one of the three that is meant specifically to serve as a FAQ platform, but if you're looking to combine a FAQ with a statistics-gathering tool, LibStats may work well for you, or, if you're also looking for software to create subject guides and database lists, SubjectsPlus is a very nice solution.

GOING FORWARD

The next chapter will take a look at the hows and whys of libraries who implemented some of the tools just introduced. Hopefully this will give you some inspiration for how you can make use of knowledge management software and strategies in your organization. It's easier than you think, and soon you'll be your library's resident knowledge management authority!

4

LIBRARY EXAMPLES AND CASE STUDIES

The following case studies take a close look at some examples of libraries that implemented various kinds of knowledge management software. Each case study will discuss how they decided upon the particular software they ended up implementing, some of the challenges they faced, and how they assessed the success of the projects. Any insights or recommendations they gleaned from the process will also be mentioned, so you don't have to reinvent the wheel, or suffer from common pitfalls or stumbling blocks. You can find the references for the full case studies in the "Recommended Reading" chapter if you'd like to learn more about the individual projects.

ENHANCING STAFF COMMUNICATION IN AN ACADEMIC LIBRARY WITH WIKIS AND BLOGS

The chief goal of a knowledge base is to collect important information from various sources, and to make that information available to all relevant parties within an organization. The easier it is to add and access the information within the knowledge base, the more likely your staff is to actively use it. In 2008, the University of Nevada, Las Vegas (UNLV), University Libraries, with a staff of over one hundred full-time employees spread out over four locations, decided to assess whether the libraries' various wikis and blogs were effective at enhancing communication among the staff. UNLV librarians Kristen Costello and Darcy Del

Bosque subsequently published their findings in a case study which gives us some important insights into using these tools to build successful knowledge bases for library staff.

A staff wiki had been launched a year earlier using MediaWiki software. The purpose of the wiki was to create an online repository for meeting minutes, policies and procedures, and departmental information. The wiki was password-protected and content was migrated from the old staff intranet to build a base of information. An alphabetically sorted table of contents, wiki policies page, how-to page, and blank template pages for standing committees were also created upon launch.

Blogs had been in use in the library since 2004, originally via the Blogger website, and later through Movable Type software. Any staff member could request an account to create their own work-related blog by filling out a form on the staff wiki. Technical support and account creation were handled by the Libraries Technologies Division, while training was tackled by the libraries' Web and Digitization Unit. Although posting was restricted to account holders with proper permissions, anyone on staff could post comments on blog entries.

In their assessment of the library's knowledge management tools, the authors found that the wiki was quite successful across the organization. It was found to be especially useful for storing and accessing information that would be needed on a regular basis. Almost all of those surveyed reported using the wiki at some point to find information, and over half of the survey respondents said they also contributed routinely. In fact, the majority of employees said they used the wiki at least once a week.

Some of the main features which led to the success of the staff wiki included pre-populating the wiki with as much content from the old staff intranet as possible, and organizing that content into categories. Providing staff with a landing page with an A-to-Z list of topics gave them an easy way to find content quickly and easily. Departments, divisions, and committees were encouraged to post their minutes and policies, and pre-built template pages were created to simplify the process. Most wiki software at this time includes a word-processing-type editing interface, so users don't have to deal with "wiki markup," which is similar to simplified version of HTML, but since this was not included in the authors' version of software by default at the time, they installed an advanced editor to make it easier for users to add and edit content.

Several of the library's blogs have attained a wide readership, including the Library News blog (which was featured on the library website's home page) and "The Dean's Blog," which was only available internally, but actively updated. Active support and participation from library administrators is a key factor to the success of any organizational project, so the dean's involvement in both the wiki and blog projects was helpful in gaining staff buy-in for the new communication channels. Also key to the projects' success were the training materials and workshops provided to staff, to help guide them through the various features of wikis and blogs, so they could make the most use of them, and easily integrate them into their current workflow.

Food for Thought: Blogs vs. Wikis

There are so many choices when it comes to website-creation software and content management systems, but if you're looking for the quickest, easiest, and cheapest way to set up a basic knowledge base for you library, blogs and wikis are probably your two best choices. When deciding which tool to implement, there are some important factors to look at which may indicate which option has the best chance of success for your specific project or purpose.

From a knowledge base perspective, both blogs and wikis work quite well to store and share information, but wikis tend to do a little better with the task of organizing that information. You have a bit more control over the organizational structure of a wiki than you do the organizational structure of a blog. Although you can set up categories within a blog in order to create an informal "table of contents," blogs are essentially organized by date rather than by topic. Even well-selected, well-curated categories in combination with the blog's search function becomes a cumbersome way to navigate content once it starts to add up, as you can have many pages of results for one category or search query. To mitigate this issue, if you decide to build your knowledge base using blogging software, policies should be considered which discuss best practices for creating concise, descriptive titles for posts, and especially for proper categorization or tagging of posts. A controlled vocabulary of topics which the posts can be tagged with may be especially helpful in organizing your content.

The nature of how people add and edit information in blogs and wikis also affects which tool will work best at your library. With a blog, when information changes, people will generally add a new post rather than editing the old post which contains that information. For this reason, a blog often becomes a repository of everything that was posted, regardless of whether that information is still valid or timely, and it can be hard to find what you are looking for amidst this clutter of information. On a wiki you would generally just edit the content to reflect the most current and up-to-date information. (It should be noted that in terms of keeping track of past changes and updates, wikis also retain the revision history of pages, which reflect edits made to that page over time.)

Despite wikis having an organizational advantage over out-of-the-box blogging software, some users may be uncomfortable with the no-frills interfaces usually found in wiki software (though this has improved over time, and you generally no longer need to know how to use wiki markup language, which is similar to HTML). Blogging platforms often have a more user-friendly interface which more closely resembles other websites that people are used to seeing and using. Setting up a blog to work effectively as a knowledge base can take a bit more customization on the administrator's part beforehand, but if it means your staff is more likely to use the tool, it may be worth it in the long run.

WORDPRESS AS A KNOWLEDGE MANAGEMENT TOOL IN TWO ACADEMIC LIBRARIES

Knowledge management is of particular importance at a library's reference desk, where a constantly shifting staff must be able to relay consistent, up-to-date information to each other, and to patrons. Collecting and providing access to this information via a knowledge management system allows anyone working at the desk to have access to the same information in order to ensure that all patrons receive the most accurate and thoroughly vetted answers to their queries.

Julia Rodriguez, the information literacy and educational technology librarian at Oakland University in Rochester, Michigan, documented her implementation of knowledge management systems built with WordPress blogging software at two different university libraries. One university chose to use WordPress.com, a hosted solution, and the other chose to install WordPress on a local server and host it themselves. When choosing between web hosting and locally hosting, she lists several factors and considerations, including:

- Time and effort: web hosting is much quicker and easier to set up and maintain, but a locally hosted site is more adaptable and scalable. If the long-run success of the project is in question, web hosting is less of a risk, because there's much less of an investment of time and effort required. You also don't have to worry about hardware with the web hosted version of WordPress.
- Access: web hosting gives some options for restricting access, but locally hosted sites have the greatest amount of authentication options, such as creating IP-restricted domains and password protection for individual posts. There are, however, plug-ins that can be installed in either version to extend the granularity of access rules without accessing the settings for the database.
- Control: customization options are limited in the web-hosted version of WordPress. Locally hosted WordPress blogs allow you full access to the code for all pages, themes, and plug-ins, making your site completely customizable. Taking full advantage of the benefits of local hosting does require an administrator with more technical knowledge though, so keep that in mind when considering this factor.

In the university library that chose the web-hosted version of Word-Press, the new knowledge base was created to build a repository of information that was traditionally communicated via e-mail or through a binder kept at the reference desk. E-mail overload and lack of organization or weeding of the binder led to a concern that important knowledge was not being efficiently recorded, preserved, and shared among the staff.

Before launching the knowledge base, guidelines for adding content were drafted and posted on the homepage of the blog, and post categories were established to help create a structure to organize future content. The new tool was announced and demonstrated at a staff meeting where training materials were also distributed. Staff response was extremely positive, and the blog provided a more organized, readily accessible way to find information and provide access to resources, as well as a place for librarians to share articles, announcements, and links.

At the second university library, the reference department already employed a digital knowledge management system, designed and hosted in-house. The system featured very limited search capabilities and no organizational structure, but did allow users to subscribe to an e-mail list which sent out updates when new notes were added. Information was also scattered across various internal websites, binders, and folders.

After installing the WordPress software on a local server, content was imported from the old system via an RSS feed import plug-in. Transitioning from one system to the other was a fairly quick and quite painless process, for both IT staff and reference desk employees. Feedback was very positive, and many users even requested that the system be expanded to include other departments besides reference.

In reflecting upon both knowledge base implementation projects, Rodriguez makes the following four recommendations for implementing new technology within an organization:

1. Clearly articulate to your potential users the benefits and broader goals of adopting the new technology. Let them know how the system will simplify their workflow not just in the short run, but also in the long run. Elaborate on how the new system is not just *replacing* an old system or workflow, but how it is *improving* upon it.
2. Eliminate barriers to adoption wherever possible. Whenever possible, do the work for your users, by creating accounts for them, presetting common preferences, and building an environment that is familiar and/or comfortable for them. If there are specific features in the system that you want your staff to use, explicitly push those features and provide training and incentives to use them.
3. Take the time to get to know your users, their workflows, and their needs, and build a system that works for them. Give them a tool which makes their jobs easier. Make sure they have plenty of opportunities for training, support, and experimentation.

4. Don't implement a system you can't support. Know the abilities of those building, launching, and supporting the system, and don't exceed their time or knowledge constraints. Make sure they have the proper tools to provide support, including access to hardware and related software systems.

Additionally, whenever attempting to introduce innovation in the workplace, whether at a technological or administrative level (or both), remember to gauge your staff's openness to change, but don't give up on change if they are resistant. Use this knowledge to strategically plan your efforts. Staff members who are resistant to change may need more support and encouragement in the early stages of implementation, but early adopters may need to be prodded to maintain high levels of engagement later down the line.

USING LIBANSWERS TO BUILD A KNOWLEDGE BASE OF COMMON REFERENCE QUESTIONS

In 2008, budget issues, reduced staff, and decreasing usage of the Research Help Desk at the University Library at Cal Poly Pomona (CPP) caused librarians to seek alternate methods of providing reference to students and faculty. The library decided to subscribe to Springshare's LibAnswers platform, which allowed them to create an easily searchable database of commonly asked questions with answers provided by librarians. Originally, librarians were tasked with coming up with questions they frequently were asked while at the Research Help Desk. Questions could also be submitted by patrons through an online form. When these questions are answered, librarians can choose to add them to the knowledge base (after removing the patron's name and contact information).

When a new question is submitted to the LibAnswers system, an e-mail can be sent to all reference librarians to ensure prompt responses (rather than reference librarians having to log into the system to see any new questions that have come in). Christy R. Stevens, in her assessment of CPP's LibAnswers implementation, notes that since you can also set the system up to copy all librarians on the eventual response to these patron-submitted questions, LibAnswers can be a valuable tool for librarians to gain new knowledge about library resources and services, and to learn from each other's reference styles.

Librarians also have the option of creating and adding topics (i.e., tags or categories) to each question. The software includes a widget (or modular piece of code) that can be added in other web locations, like on the library's website, in research guides, or in course management software like Moodle. This gave their users multiple access points to this database of frequently asked questions, or FAQ.

The LibAnswers homepage (or any of the widgets) prompts users to enter a question or keyword(s), and the system automatically generates potential matches for the question or keyword(s) as the user types. The user can then select a question from the suggestions in order to view the answer. If the system cannot find a question relevant to the user, they can either submit their question through the online form, or browse the knowledge base by topics, popular questions, or recently added questions.

During the first full year of implementation, online reference transactions at CPP increased by over 200 percent, with 71 percent of those transactions occurring through LibAnswers. Stevens points out that providing easy, 24/7 access to frequently sought information not only benefits patrons, but also frees up librarians to spend more time answering in-depth reference and research questions, as well as creating tutorials and resource guides for specific classes, departments, and subject areas, and pursuing scholarly endeavors such as article and grant-writing. She mentions directional, technology, facility, and common service questions (often called "ready reference") as the perfect type of information to include in your LibAnswers knowledge base, since librarians spend much of their time answering these questions over and over again.

LibAnswers also acts as a statistics-gathering tool, so librarians can keep track of popular questions and topics in the system. It even records search terms that don't yield any results, even if the user chooses not to submit the question for response. This feature helps point librarians toward topics that are not adequately covered in the FAQ, helping guide what information they add to the knowledge base going forward. Analyzing commonly asked questions also provides insight into what services and resources may need streamlining or rethinking, what could be made clearer through signage or on the library website, what could be more adequately covered in information literacy sessions, and suggests areas to cover in future online tutorials and guides.

FOUR CASES OF MICROSOFT SHAREPOINT ADOPTION IN SPECIAL LIBRARIES

Microsoft SharePoint is a common software solution for building intranets at libraries whose parent organization has already purchased and implemented the product, since the cost and setup will have already been covered. There are several case studies examining its implementation at academic and medical libraries in California, Maryland, and Florida which offer extremely useful insights into what can make or break a SharePoint intranet project. Given the sharp learning curve SharePoint can present (as will be discussed in the following chapter on implementation) it makes sense to think carefully about your organization's needs and spend some time in the planning stages to decide if SharePoint is right for your library and your staff.

The nice thing about Microsoft SharePoint is that it offers much of the functionality of a content management system like Drupal or WordPress without the need for programming skills. Because it is built to be inward-facing (i.e., it's designed to be used by internal staff who have the proper credentials to log in), it also has many security and privacy features that need to be added or custom-built into other content management systems, which were designed to build outward-facing websites (i.e., visible to anyone on the open web.) The *problem* with Microsoft SharePoint is that it offers so many features and options that it can be daunting to set up and to use. Because most librarians don't have the time or resources to conduct an in-depth analysis of their staff to assess their needs and website design preferences, it is wise to make use of the case studies that have been done on the topic to best design an intranet that will be useful and, more importantly, *used*.

SharePoint as a Reference Department Intranet at an Academic Library

David Dahl, emerging technologies librarian at Towson University in Maryland, chronicled his library's 2008 adoption of Microsoft Share-Point as their Reference Department's intranet, which they called the RefPortal. The RefPortal was intended to facilitate communication among the library's reference staff, disseminate information, and provide a central location for storing and collaborating on documents such as policies and procedures. One of the goals of the RefPortal was to replace communication via e-mail, and make policies and procedures available via a shared network drive and print documentation via a binder kept at the reference desk.

When assessing available tools, the two most important functions of the new system were facilitating communication and building an easily accessible knowledge base. The library looked into wikis, blogs, home-grown intranet systems, and open source software, but in the end decided that a wiki or a blog would not support all the functionality they desired in an intranet, and home-grown or open-source systems would require too much time in the planning and development stages. The university's timely adoption of SharePoint on an organizational level clinched the library's decision to use this out-of-the-box solution.

The RefPortal was built to easily facilitate four main tasks, which included:

1. recording reference transaction statistics via SharePoint's Site Aggregator app (to embed their StatsTracker tool, already in use);
2. posting announcements via SharePoint's Announcements app;
3. storing and retrieving procedures and policies via SharePoint's Wiki Library app; and
4. reporting computing and printing issues via SharePoint's Issue Tracker app.

The four apps were added to the RefPortal, and then those Web Parts were added to the RefPortal homepage for easy viewing and access. Upon logging in, users could immediately see the five latest announcements, five newest issues, and five most recent wiki edits, as well as the interface for logging new reference transactions into the system. Announcements and issues were set to be removed from the list once their set expiration date passed, or the issue was marked as resolved.

Dahl marks several factors as contributing to the success of the Ref-Portal, including the integration of the already-in-use StatsTracker into the new system. Since they were required to use StatsTracker when on the reference desk, the desktop and browser links to access it just needed to be changed to the new RefPortal. While logged into the RefPortal to use StatsTracker, staff was exposed to the other features in the new intranet system, and gradually began using them. Dahl comments that "functions that are necessary for job performance will guarantee increased use of the intranet if they are strategically embedded within it."

Dahl also recommends pre-populating sections of SharePoint in order to serve both as examples of appropriate content, and to draw users into using those sections. For the wiki library section of the RefPortal, an index and table of contents were added ahead of time, as well as a guide for properly creating and editing wiki content.

A year and a half after implementing the RefPortal, the library conducted a survey to assess user satisfaction. They used SharePoint's own built-in survey application to collect the data, which found that the reference staff was still actively using the RefPortal, that they were satisfied with the software, and that they found it a very useful tool.

SharePoint as a Medical Library Online Portal

In 2009 Judith Kammerer, the medical librarian at the Community Regional Medical Center in Fresno, California, conducted a case study of her involvement with her hospital system's implementation of Microsoft SharePoint, specifically about the creation of the library's Share-Point portal. In this case study, the library moved all of their online content into SharePoint, thus replacing their previous website. The project took eight months, and was part of a system-wide SharePoint implementation that involved the system's IT staff and also web developers. Because of this project's scope and resources it presents a fairly unique case, but yielded two very useful insights into successful implementation strategies for libraries involved in a system-wide SharePoint deployment project.

1. If your library's parent organization has just recently acquired or decided upon using Microsoft SharePoint, get a librarian in at the earliest possible planning stages. System design decisions made for top-level sites will influence subsites and limit what you are able to do with your portal, so make sure the library's voice is heard!

2. Training is a major factor in getting your staff to actively use any new software product, so reach out to your IT department or whoever is in charge of SharePoint implementation and training at your organization to obtain as much documentation and training materials as possible. Make training materials available in a variety of formats, including videos, tutorials with screenshots, and in-person training sessions, so new users can learn the system in the method that best suits their schedule and learning style.

This project demonstrates that Microsoft SharePoint is a very viable option for building websites, especially if they are for an internal audience, and require special security measures or user permissions. The available training materials and add-ons create a great environment for website administrators who are looking to learn and grow their skills along with the site.

SharePoint for Document Management at a Distance Education Academic Library

In 2010, University of Maryland librarians Jennifer Diffin, Fanuel Chirombo, Dennis Nangle, and Mark de Jong published a case study on the implementation of Microsoft SharePoint by the document management team at the University of Maryland University College (a branch of the University of Maryland comprised mostly of distance education students.) The document management team provides circulation and interlibrary loan services to the college, and had experienced a rapid growth period over the course of several years, leading to knowledge gaps.

In the past, documentation had been kept in print format, binders, and also on a shared network drive, but without a formalized process information became spread out across multiple binders in multiple locations, and across multiple personal folders and directories in the shared drive, without any surefire way to locate and identify the most recent, definitive version of each document. The team researched and tested several knowledge base systems, including a home-grown, web-based manual and a wiki, but neither fully met their team's need for a centralized system for communication, collaboration, and document storage with a focus on eliminating redundancy and knowledge gaps. The team eventually decided upon Microsoft SharePoint as a software solution because it was already installed and managed at the institutional level by the university's IT department, and because it could combine the team's disparate technology systems, including a wiki, a calendaring system, and a document repository, all into one centralized portal.

Over the course of the implementation and testing process, some best practices were established that will be useful to other library's embarking upon a SharePoint project.

- A document was created with guidelines for naming conventions, document retention, and appropriate use of SharePoint applications.
- The team's documentation was carefully weeded and files were renamed as necessary to fit the new naming convention guidelines before migrating them into SharePoint.
- The wiki structure was decided upon and built and the wiki was pre-populated with a table of contents, style guide, and content from the team's previous wikis before the site was officially launched.
- E-mail alerts were set up to notify staff of changes in SharePoint, such as document or wiki additions or edits.
- Users were shown how to map SharePoint as a network drive on their computer, giving them another option for accessing Share-Point documents and wiki pages besides going through their Internet browser.

The project was a huge success, streamlining the team's workflow and improving communication and productivity. Usage has consistently risen since the launch, and user satisfaction has led to the software's implementation among several other departments and teams. The library was even lauded by the school's IT department for its innovation, and held up as a model for future SharePoint adoption by other university departments.

SharePoint in a Small Academic Library

In her article "Organizational and Social Factors in the Adoption of Intranet 2.0: A Case Study" published in 2010, Bohyun Kim discusses how the Florida International University (FIU) Medical Library launched and assessed the usage of their SharePoint intranet. She focuses particularly on the social aspects of SharePoint, why those social tools were underused, and how organizational and social factors can play a vital part in active contribution and collaboration within intranets.

The Medical Library is a department within FIU's College of Medicine (COM), and it was the COM IT Department that chose and installed SharePoint to create the college's intranet. Select departments within the college, including the Medical Library, were then contacted and encouraged to create subsites within the system. IT also provided guidance for each department for structuring and organizing their new sites.

Within the library, the digital access librarian, with the help of IT's system administrator, was tasked with building the library's SharePoint site. Since both the library and the college were entirely new entities, with much of their staff yet to be hired and workflows not yet established, building the site was a unique challenge. Its original incarnation had seven pages: the library intranet homepage, cataloging and collections, digital access services, education, help desk, interlibrary loan, and reference. Links to each page were located at the top of each page, and each page had the following web parts: announcements, links, document library, and discussion forum. The calendar, picture library, survey, task list, and RSS viewer web parts were also added to select pages. All staff members were entered into the system with the contribute permission level, allowing everyone to view, add, and update content.

Upon launch, the library's intranet was immediately put to use for two major projects: collaborating on library policies via a document library, and brainstorming the structure, content, and design of the library's public website, using a wiki library. Both projects successfully made use of the software, and the library staff were highly satisfied with

SharePoint as a new way to store and share documents. They preferred it over the former shared network drive because they could access work files from home more easily, and could share documents and folders using fairly sophisticated permissions.

Microsoft SharePoint is an extremely powerful and feature-rich knowledge management solution, but cost and learning curve can be intimidating to some potential users. However, if it is the software package most likely to solve all your internal communication and resource management with one tool, so it can be more than worth the effort if it's right for your organization. Some important questions to ask when considering SharePoint include:

- Does your parent organization use the product, helping to alleviate the burdens of cost, setup, and training?
- How quickly does the intranet/knowledge base need to be deployed? Will there be time for proper strategic planning, software customization, and pre-population of content? (*Note*: Kim's case study also mentions user expectations. SharePoint can have a less sleek appearance than many external websites if deployed "out of the box," leading to lower user satisfaction and, ultimately, usage.)
- Are there people on staff who will volunteer to champion the project? Your implementation is more likely to succeed if you have people who are willing to give you feedback, help other users, and keep the content of the intranet fresh.
- Will it make your staff's jobs easier? If they're perfectly happy with their current workflow, they will be reluctant to adopt a new tool. The benefit of SharePoint is that it has the capability to combine access to disparate systems into one portal, so make it worth their while to log in and interact with the new software by embedding tools and resources they would normally access separately, or by adding useful new tools that were previously unavailable to staff.
- How comfortable is your staff with new technology? Although most users in these case studies found SharePoint fairly easy to use, comfort with technology can vary widely among workplaces. Users more familiar with interactive and social features on websites are more likely to add and edit content in an intranet. Train-

ing materials and assistance should be readily available in a variety of forms for users who encounter problems.

5

STEP-BY-STEP LIBRARY PROJECTS

The previous chapters have introduced some knowledge management tools and techniques and discussed how libraries are successfully making use of them. This section will outline some practical projects which you can implement at your own library. Whether your library is large or small, academic, public, or special—or even if you're a solo librarian—there's something for everyone here, so let's get started!

HOW TO CREATE A DOCUMENT MANAGEMENT SYSTEM WITH GOOGLE DRIVE

Colleagues often need to share and collaborate on documents and spreadsheets. After a file is created, the creator will often send it to coworkers via e-mail. It is then up to each recipient to keep track of the file, and to resend it whenever edits are made. Because each person has their own copy of the file, which they can edit at will, this quickly leads to the existence of many versions of the same file. Google Drive is a free and easy way to share and collaborate on documents without all the e-mail attachment hassle.

Some organizations try to solve the multiple copy problem by having a shared space on a local server where "official" versions of library files like reports, brochures, minutes, and handouts can be stored. Often, employees have trouble remembering how to access the shared space, which is usually by "mapping" the location as a drive on their computer, or accessing the server through a File Transfer Protocol (FTP) application. Both of these methods can also be problematic when employees try to access the files from their home computers. Google Drive can be used to replace your shared network space, alleviating the need for self-hosting of files, and allowing staff to access their work files from anyplace with an internet connection.

Getting Organized

Google Drive is designed to act a lot like the folders on your own computer, so it makes sense to take some time to organize your documents before you upload them onto the site. Download all of the documents off of your shared drive into a folder on your own computer. Within that folder, create sub-folders, either for the different kind of documents you'll be storing there (reports, promotional items, statistics, etc.), or by department (Reference, Circulation, Interlibrary Loan, etc.).

If you feel your current organizational scheme works well, it is best not to deviate too much from it, since this is what people are already used to. If you are not happy with the current organization, or if all the files are just in one folder, then this is the perfect time to sort out all your files so they will be easy for other staff members to find. Remember that you can nest folders within folders, so you can have a "Reports" folder in each departmental folder, or vice versa, but remember the deeper a file is buried in folders, the harder it will be to find. (Although Google Drive does have a great search feature which will make things easier to find, easier than they ever were on your shared drive.)

Uploading Folders and Files

First you will need to sign up for a Google account. This does not mean that you need a Gmail account; you can sign up for a Google account with any e-mail address. Once you are signed into Google Drive, you can choose to either create a new document from scratch, or you can upload a document you've already created in Microsoft Word, Excel, PowerPoint, or other popular software product. Since you've already sorted your files into folders, you can actually just upload each folder, so there's no need to upload each individual file (see figure 5.1).

Its powerful search function is one of the great features of Google Drive, and there are a few things you can do to make your newly added files easier to find. For documents that will be accessed frequently, you can mark them as important by right-clicking on the file or folder, and then clicking "Add star." You can view a list of all your starred documents via the navigation on the left side of the page. (Stars can later be removed in the same way they are added.)

You can also add some metadata to a file or folder by clicking on it, and then clicking the "information" icon at the top of the page to reveal the details and activity pane for that item. Under the details tab is a section marked with a pencil icon, which says "Add a description." Click on the icon to add keywords, a summary, abstract, or other metadata to help users locate and identify the item.

Sharing and Collaborating

When you are ready to share a folder or file with colleagues, use the "Share" button in the upper right-hand corner of your screen. By default, your document is set as *Private*, and is visible only to you, the creator. If you click on the link to change the access settings, you will see there are three visibility options: *Public on the web*, which allows anyone on the Internet to view the file, without signing into a Google account; *Anyone with the link*, which also doesn't require a sign-in to view, but is only accessible through the specific link that you create; and *Shared privately*, which makes the file accessible only to specific users, who you add by entering their e-mail addresses in the "Invite people" area at the bottom of the original *Sharing settings* dialog box (see figure 5.2)

There are a few things you should be aware of when sharing folders and files:

1. When sharing the link, be sure to use the link listed in the *Share settings* dialog box. Do not simply copy and paste the link from your Internet browser's URL bar. The links are slightly different, and using the wrong one sometimes triggers a log-in prompt, even if you have the document visibility on a setting that does not require sign-in.

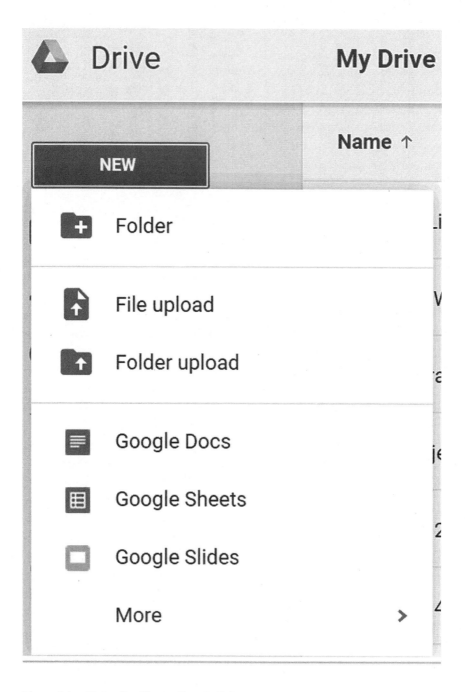

Figure 5.1.   Uploading files to Google Drive

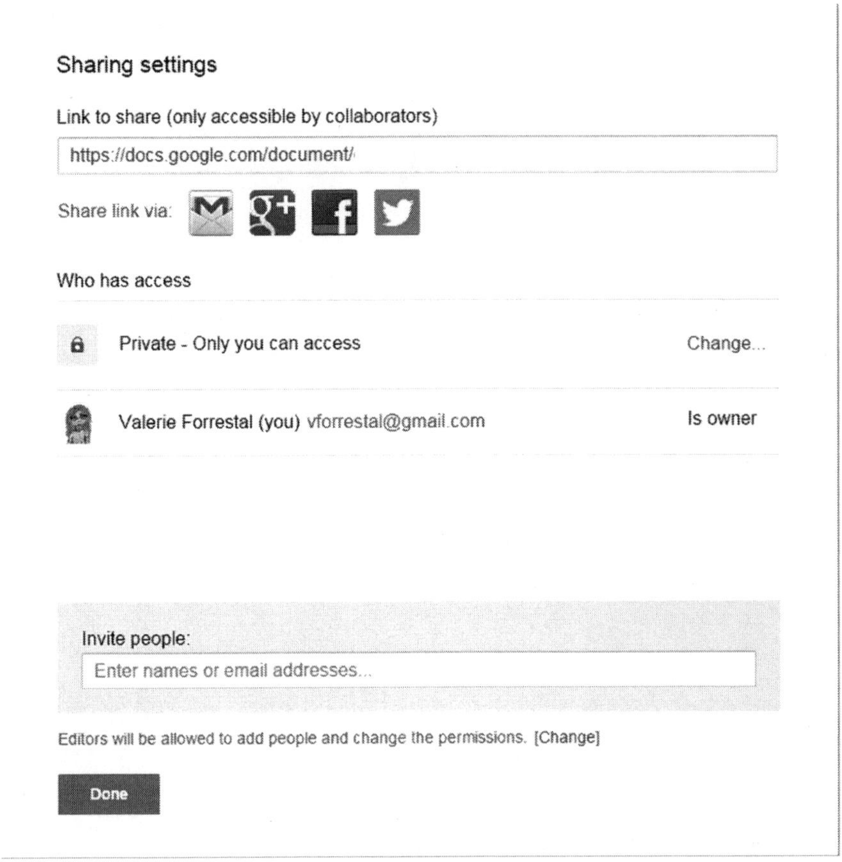

Figure 5.2.   Available sharing settings for files in Google Drive

2. Be aware that using the *Anyone with the link* setting does not necessarily limit the accessibility of your document. Once you send the link to other users, they may further distribute it via e-mail or may publish it to the web.

3. If you share a folder, all documents in that folder are shared, and new documents created will have those same sharing settings. You must manually change the settings of individual or new files if you do not want them to be automatically shared.

4. A document's web link remains the same even if you move it into or out of a folder, or move it from one folder to another.

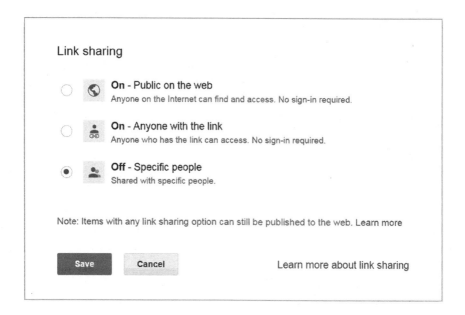

Figure 5.3.

Once your files are uploaded into Google Drive and shared with the appropriate colleagues, you can start using it not just for storage, but for collaboration. Now your staff can work together on documents in the cloud without creating the multiple-version problem or having to constantly send comments and updates via e-mail. To get the most out of collaborating in Google Drive, you should familiarize yourself with the following features, explained in detail below:

- Sharing settings
- Permission levels
- File versioning
- Activity tracking
- Optical character recognition

Collaborators and Permission Levels

The creator of a file is known as the "Owner," and they can edit or delete the file, invite or remove access from other users, transfer ownership to another user, and add or remove files from folders. When you share a file or folder with other users, you can designate them as "Editors," "Viewers," or "Commenters."

By default, Editors can add or remove other users (except for the Owner) and change the visibility options of a file or folder. You can change this in the *Sharing settings* dialog box, under the "Invite people" section. Editors can also download and sync documents to their own devices, add and remove items from folders, and view the complete list of collaborators for a file or folder. They cannot permanently delete a file or folder.

Viewers and Commenters can only view, download, copy, and sync files and folders that are shared with them, with Commenters having the added ability to add comments to files.

Keeping Track of File Versions

With multiple people editing the same file, it's important to be able to track activity and view older versions of files. For example, if you haven't opened a document in a while, you may want to see what changes have been made to it since the last time you read it, and who has been working on it. To toggle the activity panel on or off, click the information button in the top right corner of the Google Drive screen (look for an "i" in a circle). By default, the panel will show all activity for all files and folders, including moving, removing, renaming, uploading, sharing or unsharing, editing and commenting. It will also tell you the user who made the change, and the date and time of the activity. You can narrow the activity log to specific files or folders by checking the box to the left of the item in the main file/folder list. When tracking the activity for individual files and folders, you can also switch the activity panel to "Details" view, where you can quickly view and edit its metadata and sharing options.

To see what changes have been made to a file over time, and who has made those changes, open the file and click on "See revision history" under the File menu. This will toggle on a panel on the right side of your screen showing various versions of that file. A version is created every time the document auto saves, and you can use this panel to roll back the document to any of these previous versions. By default, however, the panel will show only the versions wherein major changes were made. To see all revisions click on "Show more detailed revisions" at the bottom of the panel.

Each person who has made edits to the document will be shown in a different color within the revision history panel. When you click on a previous version of the document in the revision history panel, any text that was changed since the preceding revision will be shown in the color that corresponds with the person who made the edits, so you can easily see what changes that person made to the document. Google automatically deletes old versions of files that are over thirty days old or when the file has reached one hundred revisions. If you want to permanently save a particular revision of a file, go to the File menu and select "Make a copy." *Note*: Older versions of Google Drive allowed you to compare specific revisions of a document to each other, but the current version does not have this functionality. If you want to see all of the changes that have been made to a document since the last time you viewed it, you'll have to scroll through the revisions from your last save forward, or install an add-on like "Track Changes" (www.letterfeed.zendesk.com).

Text documents in Google Drive also give users a way to make comments or suggest edits without changing the actual text of the document. These are excellent features to use when you want to solicit feedback on a report or review while still retaining authorship of the document. To add a comment to a document, select the text you'd like to leave a comment about, and click the *Comments* button in the upper right-hand corner of the screen. To suggest edits which the file owner can then accept or reject, click on the *Editing* button in the top right corner of the screen, under *Comments*, and switch it to *Suggesting* mode. You can also use the *Comments* button to reply to a suggested edit, explain why you either accepted or rejected it, or to reply to and resolve comments.

Optical Character Recognition

You can also use Google Drive to OCR your PDF or image files. OCR stands for *optical character recognition* and is the process of using a computer algorithm to extract text from a non-text file so that it can be searched or so that text can be copied from that document. When running these algorithms on your original file, Google creates a new Google document version of the file, and attempts to match the new file as closely to the original as possible. Formatting elements like font size and type, line breaks, and bold and italic text can be retained in most cases, but some structural elements like lists, tables, columns, footnotes, and endnotes may be lost. For best results, Google recommends that the text in your PDF or image be at least 10 pixels high, of horizontal, left-to-right orientation, and in common fonts like Arial or Times New Roman. Images should be sharp, with even lighting and clear contrast.

The OCR function makes Google Drive a great tool for digitally storing old library documents like reports or meeting minutes. First, scan and save them as a JPEG or PDF document. Then, when you upload them into Drive, make sure to check the box that says "Convert text from PDF and image files to Google documents." It's that simple to turn those old file folders full of documents into a searchable digital repository.

Using Google Drive for Marketing and Promotions

Not only is Google Drive a good place to store library documents, but it can also help make your brochures and flyers for library services and events easier to share and promote. When you send promotional materials out as e-mail attachments, you're not giving recipients an easy way to share the information without having to forward the e-mail to others. Many people would perhaps rather share the information on their social media accounts, which can be a hassle with a large PDF or image file.

When you promote your next library event, upload the flyer to Google Drive and save it as *Public on the web*, which will create a URL that which you can include in your e-mails, and that your patrons can share in whatever way they choose. You can even use a URL-shortening service like TinyURL (www.tinyurl.com) or Bitly (www.bitly.com) to give your flyer a custom link that is easy to remember and share.

You are now ready to create, share, and collaborate on documents in Google Drive! Remember, not only is Google Drive a great collaboration tool, but you can also access those files from anywhere with an Internet connection, so go ahead and work from home today!

HOW TO CONSTRUCT A WEB-BASED KNOWLEDGE BASE USING WIKI SOFTWARE

Wikis are not a new technology, nor have they changed all that much over the years. This simplicity is a strength and not a weakness. Adding features to a piece of software usually makes it more difficult to use, and sometimes it's best to just do a few things and do them well.

Learning the basics of how wikis work can be a useful skill, as wikis are often included in other kinds of communication and collaboration software like content management systems and intranets. In fact, Commons in a Box and Microsoft SharePoint, which will be discussed later in the chapter, both have wiki software included in them as a way to provide users with easy collaborative spaces.

Wikis: An Overview

So what exactly is a wiki, and what can it do? A wiki is basically a collaborative website, and its chief purpose is to provide an online space for people to work together on documentation. Wikis are usually used to collect and share information about an event, project, or organization (or specific department within an organization). Wikis are extremely versatile and can be used to store files, share links, and embed media such as images and video. A wiki can act as an openly accessible website or a private intranet. Unlike Google Drive, which mimics the file structure of a personal computer, a wiki looks more like a website, so it is better for projects that have information that is best structured with separate pages linked by persistent navigation.

Wiki software can be installed on your own server, or you can use a cloud-based platform like PBworks. This project will utilize a cloud-based service, because it is the quickest and easiest to set up, but if you choose to host your own wiki, editing and administrating the wiki is basically the same once the software is installed and running.

Creating an Online Policies and Procedures Manual with PBworks

Wikis are a great way to get those library policies and procedures that are scattered in binders and folders at the reference and circulation desk organized and in one central location. Once you've gathered your policies and procedures together, group them into logical categories or topics. These categories will become the individual pages of your wiki.

To get started building your wiki, you must first create a PBworks account and set up your wiki workspace. The PBworks website offers various kinds of free and paid accounts. Librarians can take advantage of their free *Education Hub*, which offers a greater number of users and a higher storage limit than their other account options. You can only create one wiki workspace per educational account, so if you need an individual wiki for several departments, events, or projects, you can either use their *Project Hub* or assign different users as creators for each wiki. Once a person creates a wiki, they can add other users as administrators for that workspace. *Note*: Ownership of a workspace can be transferred, but only by e-mailing PBworks directly from the e-mail address used to create the workspace.

To create a new PBworks wiki, go to www.PBworks.com and click on *Get Started* in the upper right-hand corner of the page. Select *EDU-Hub* from the following screen, and then select *Basic* from the available account types. You will be prompted to choose a URL for your work-space in the following format: *http://YOUR_WORKSPACE_NAME .pbworks.com*. If you choose to make your workspace openly available on the Internet, this is the link you will use to share the wiki, so choose a name that is descriptive but concise. It is also the link that shows up in a user's list of available wikis when they sign into PBworks, so choosing a descriptive name is also important for wikis that are privately shared.

Once your workspace is set up, you can start creating pages for your policies and procedures. To create a new page in PBworks, click on the *Pages & Files* tab at the top of the page, and then click the *New* button. Click the link to the page to open it, then click the *EDIT* tab to add content. PBworks allows users to add content in a word-processor-like setting, so inserting lists, links, and tables is quite easy. Here are some things to think about when transferring content from whatever the old system (whether hard-copy or digital) to the new wiki:

- Too many pages will cause site sprawl, which can confuse users, but jamming too much content into individual pages will make them hard to read and navigate, so a balance between the two must be found.

- Break large content chunks up into sections wherever possible, so the user is not faced with massive blocks of text.
- Insert placeholders for images. Many people are visual learners, so screenshots can be very helpful to users, but for the sake of getting the content transferred quickly and efficiently, you can always create and add these screenshots later.

Once you've created pages and populated them with all your policies and procedures, it's time to customize your wiki's homepage so that when users access the knowledge base, they are able to quickly and easily find what they are looking for. Your wiki homepage should give users an idea of the kind of content found in the wiki, and help guide them quickly and easily to the information they are seeking. Think of this landing page as a kind of table of contents for the wiki, which sorts pages into topics or lists them alphabetically. Since a wiki is a rather loose collection of web pages, this is the place to give your knowledge base some structure and organization. It is also useful to start the homepage off with a welcome message or statement of purpose, which defines the scope of the knowledge base, and gives some basic tips or guidelines for its use.

Another important feature of a wiki is the sidebar. The sidebar can be edited like any other page in your workspace, but displays as a small box to the side of every regular page in the wiki. Because the sidebar is always visible, it is usually used for navigational links, allowing users to easily locate and navigate to the main areas of your site.

Sidebar Tips

- It should always be simple for a user to get from whatever page they are on, back to the homepage, as well as any other important or frequently visited pages (like the wiki guidelines or FAQ page, for example).
- You can also use your sidebar for directions, disclaimers, or copyright information that you would like to always have visible to your users, or to link to relevant files or documents.
- *Note*: In the free version of PBworks you cannot delete or rename the sidebar, or add extra sidebar content boxes to your wiki.

Finally, it's a good idea to create a page with directions for using the wiki, as well as best practices. Remember that a wiki is built for collaboration, so ideally you will have more than one user adding and editing content. This makes it important to have some consistency in the layout and organization of new pages. Specify whether you'd like contributors to include screenshots, and if so, how to create them. Create guidelines on the minimum and maximum sizes for images. If your pages have a very specific structure, you can even create page templates so your users don't have to start from scratch when adding a page.

Creating Page Templates

Let's say you want all your procedures pages to include the following sections:

- description of procedure;
- step by step instructions;
- department/staff procedure applies to; and
- contact person for questions/comments.

To create a template which others can then use for new procedures pages with those sections already included, just create a new page and add the sections and any dividers or formatting elements. Once your page is set up so that users can just fill in content into the sections you've created, click on "Add Tags" in the box on the right side of the page, and type "template" into the box. Now when a user creates a new page, they will see an option to "Use a template," under which there will be a drop down list of all the templates you've created (in this case you might have one for policies and one for procedures).

Embedding Images in Your Pages

Images help break up large blocks of text and help users visualize a process or a task. In order to add an image to a page, you must first upload that image to *Pages & Files*. You can then insert the cursor wherever you'd like the image to appear, and click *Add Link* in the formatting menu (see figure 5.4).

Notes on using images:

- The image must be saved as a PNG, JPEG, or GIF for it to be displayed. Other file formats will appear as a link, and the user will need the appropriate software to view it.
- You can crop, or edit the height, width, margins, or alignment of a displayed image by right-clicking on it, or go directly to the *Edit Image* options by double-clicking.
- If you rename a file in the file list after it has been added to a page or pages, those links will no longer work, and the images will no longer display. You can double-click on the image to edit the filename, or delete and re-add the image.

Creating Training Materials or a How-To Page for Your Staff

Many of the case studies show that while library staff members find wiki knowledge bases incredibly useful for storing and finding information, they can initially be intimidated about contributing to it. The following is a list of concepts which you can add to your training materials and to the instructional page of your wiki to help them feel confident navigating, editing, and actively building upon the knowledge base:

- All wiki pages have two tabs (see figure 5.5): *VIEW* and *EDIT*. Click on the *edit* tab to add or edit content on that page. When in edit mode, a page appears much like a text document, with a

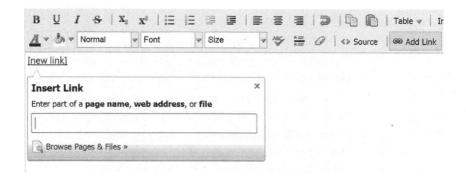

Figure 5.4. Adding images via the Insert Link dialog

menu that allows you to format your text with font style choices, as well as menu items for inserting links and embeddable media.

- When you make changes to a page, be sure to click *Save* at the bottom of the screen. Navigating away from a page you are working on (or switching back to the *VIEW* tab) without saving it will cause your changes to be lost.
- The *Wiki* tab at the top of the page takes you to your workspace's landing page. Whatever page you are on, clicking on this tab will always return you to the homepage.
- The *Pages & Files* tab allows you to see all of the webpages which make up your wiki, and is also where you create pages and upload files. In addition, in this tab you can create folders and move files into folders to help you organize your content.

Figure 5.5. Wiki navigation tabs in PBworks

Adding Users to Your Wiki

Once you've created your wiki and populated with all the content as discussed above, it's time to add your colleagues as users so they can view, comment on, and contribute to the knowledge base. The *Users* tab at the top of the page shows who has access to the wiki, and allows you to add new users or assign roles to users. The role assigned to a user determines what changes, if any, they can make to the wiki. For example, you can allow department managers to have full control over what is posted or deleted from the wiki, with full-time workers able to edit but not delete pages, and part-time workers able to only view but not change any of the content. In PBworks, you can assign the following roles to users, granting them the associated permissions within the wiki:

- *Administrator*: can view and edit all content in the workspace, add and delete pages and files, and can change the workspace's settings
- *Editor*: can view and edit all content in the workspace, add and delete pages and files, but do not have access to the workspace's settings
- *Writer*: can view and edit content, add pages and files, but cannot delete pages or files
- *Reader*: can only view content in the workspace and download uploaded files, but cannot edit content or upload new files

Tip: to set more specific permission levels, move pages into folders, and set specific permissions for those folders. For example, you can create a folder for each department's policies and procedures, and assign departmental staff as administrators, editors, or writers, with non-departmental staff as readers, so they can only view those pages. This way every department can only make changes to their own pages.

Keeping Track of Edits and Activity on Your Wiki

Finally, like Google Drive, your wiki contains a *Recent Activity* tracker. Your recent activity will always appear in a box to the side of your pages. This box contains the activity for the entire workspace, including pages created, edited, renamed, or deleted, folders created, renamed, or deleted, and files uploaded or renamed. *Note*: the *Recent Activity* tracker does not show files that have been deleted.

To view an individual page's edits, first click on the page. The person who last edited the page, and the time and date of those edits, will appear under the page title. To view the complete history of the page's edits, click on the *Page history* link in the upper right-hand corner of a page, when it is in view mode. Page history will give you a list of the page's revisions, along with an option to compare any two versions of the page, or delete specific revisions (see figure 5.6). You can also revert the page back to any of its displayed revisions, by clicking on it, and then clicking *Revert to this version* on the top of the page.

You're now set to get started on creating a wiki of your own! Create one for your reference librarians, with a schedule and important information, for that committee you're on, or even for your next library

> ⊘ **This version was saved 4 minutes ago** | Saved by 🔒 Valerie Forrestal
> View current version   Revert to this version   Page history | on March 10, 2015 at 3:59:33 pm

Figure 5.6.   Page history and revision control in PBworks

event. If you run into any trouble along the way, PBworks has an online manual specifically for educational wiki users at http://edumanual. pbworks.com (and it's a wiki, of course)!

HOW TO SET UP A PRIVATE SOCIAL NETWORK FOR YOUR STAFF WITH YAMMER

Love them or hate them, social networking sites have become ubiquitous. Users have become accustomed to communicating via "status updates" and "wall posts." If you're looking for a tool which creates that same feeling of community and social interaction, Yammer might just be for you. Yammer allows you to create an organizational social network that enables coworker interaction via instant messaging, status updates, private messaging, shared documents, announcements, and polls. You can also create and post events, and even give colleagues a virtual high five with a multitude of available digital badges. Yammer also has a directory of applications such as an organizational chart builder, leaderboards, goal trackers, and mobile apps for Android, iPhone, iPad, and Windows Phones.

Getting Started

To get started with Yammer, you will have to create an account on www.yammer.com with your organizational e-mail. This is how Yammer ensures that users who want to join your network are members of your institution. If you are creating a network for a department within a larger institution, you may find that the institution already has a Yammer network setup. In this case, you can create a group within the larger network (see figure 5.7). Groups can be internal, meaning all users must have the same organizational e-mail, or external, meaning you can invite outside collaborators into the group. Internal groups can be public or private, however, public does not mean they can be accessed by anyone on the Internet, only that they can be viewed by anyone within the larger network. External groups can be open, meaning any group members can invite new users to the group, or closed, meaning only group administrators can invite new members.

Notifications

Because of its portal-style interface, Yammer is an excellent tool for communicating with staff who don't necessarily interact in person on a regular basis. There is a notifications tab which will show any activity since you last logged in, so you can easily track updates, announcements, or events that have been posted. The event feature also has an

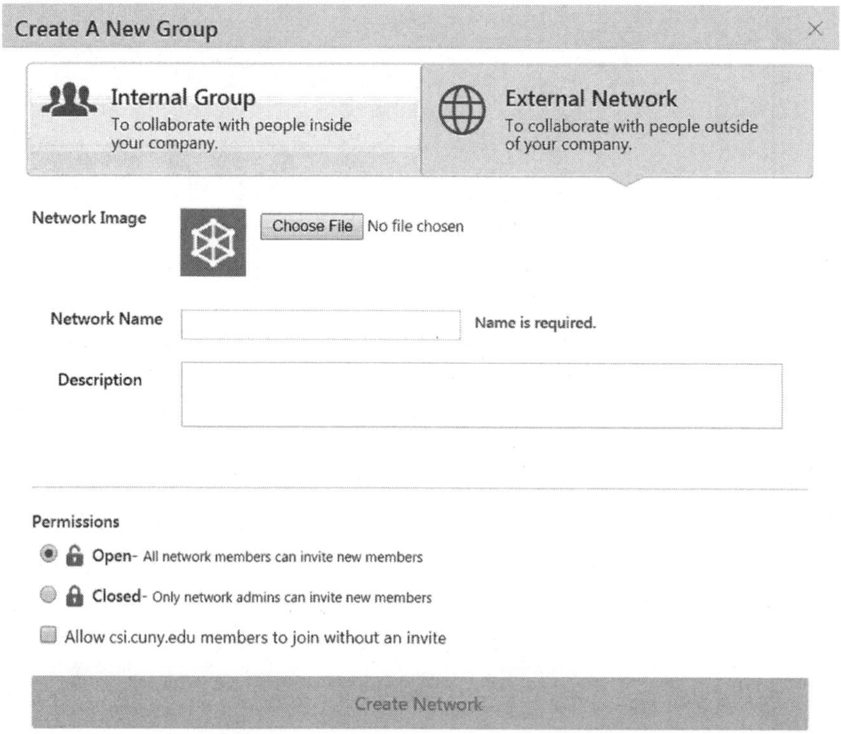

Figure 5.7. Creating groups in Yammer

RSVP function, as well as the ability to export an event to your calendar software, including Outlook, Google Calendar, or iCal.

You can edit what e-mail notifications you receive by clicking on the ellipsis in the upper right corner of Yammer. In the drop down menu, select "Edit Profile." From there, select "Notifications," choose an available network, and check the boxes for the Yammer activities and groups about which you'd like to receive notifications. You can also use this page to set up a daily or weekly e-mail digest of activity.

Group admins can also post announcements, add group information, or pin files to the group homepage. When a user logs in, all of their groups will be listed on the left-hand side of the page, under their photo. When they click on a group, they can view the group's feed, or click the tabs at the top of the feed to view any files or notes shared by the group. To the left of their feed they will see any announcements or pinned items, as well as the access options for the group. Within the access options you can leave a group, subscribe to its updates via e-mail, or get the code to embed the group into a different website or piece of software.

Sharing and Commenting on Documents

You can also upload and share documents from your Yammer home-page. After logging in, just click the *Add a Doc/Image* link above the *Update* box. Yammer's document viewing feature does not allow you to make edits directly to the text, so it is better for sharing documents that you want comments on, but that you don't want people to be able to directly edit. The commenting options are very visual and allow users to draw freehand on the document, to highlight or cross out lines, and to insert point or area comments that relate to one spot or a box of text. Please note, when you download documents, they will not retain the comments in Microsoft Word. However, when you re-upload a document that has notes or comments made in Yammer (keeping the same file name) those notes and comments will still be available in the updated document.

Socializing and Customizing Your Network

Like many other social networks, Yammer allows users to "like," comment on, and share updates. Additionally, you can bookmark, add *Topics* (or tags), and e-mail updates to yourself. These features are important because Yammer is more ephemeral than other knowledge bases, and focuses more on timely communication than on building a cache of knowledge, so it's important to give your users a way to find the information later in whatever way best suits their workflow. In this way you can push as much content as possible and allow each user to build their own custom knowledge base of information relevant specifically to them. Because you are building your knowledge base through natural communication and interaction, you'll find that the content builds up quickly and effortlessly! Users can also "follow" topics, so anything tagged with that topic will show up in a user's feed. This becomes especially important as your network grows, since the amount of information a user has access to might start to feel overwhelming to them. You cannot create a controlled vocabulary for topics, but once you add a topic to a post, it is stored in the Topics App, allowing users to search already created topics when they tag an update. You can also view all available topics in the Topics App, as well as follow or unfollow them.

As a group or network admin, encourage your users to maintain a current profile, including uploading a profile picture. By adding a picture, contact information, areas of expertise, and interests, coworkers can easily find and communicate with possible collaborators. Yammer allows users to add their other communication and social network information as well, including Twitter, Skype, LinkedIn, Facebook, and outside instant messaging clients. Contact information, expertise, and interests appear in the *Info* box on the right side of a user's profile page. Users can also add their work and educational background via the built-in forms at the bottom of their *Edit Profile* page. A user's work and educational background can be found on the *Info* tab within their profile pages.

One of the nice things about Yammer is that it greatly supports interaction between coworkers who might not normally communicate. Browse your network and groups for coworkers with shared interests or expertise which could be relevant to projects you are working on. Post regular updates about your projects, general questions you have regarding other departments, or thoughts on the field in general. This can spark creative thinking and inspiration by garnering input from new parties, and helps facilitate what is known as *cross-pollination of ideas*. It can be extremely helpful to have a fresh set of eyes on your project or workflow.

HOW TO CREATE AN ORGANIZATIONAL COMMONS WITH WORDPRESS

If you'd like to enable and encourage your coworkers and employees to have their own spaces to create and share content, Commons in a Box is for you! Commons in a Box (CBOX) is a project by the City University of New York and the CUNY Graduate Center that makes it easy to turn WordPress into an online commons for your organization. Users can create profiles, blogs, and groups so staff members can create a blog for their department, a group with discussion boards for their project, or just network by linking profiles.

To get your CBOX site up and running, you will need a local installation of WordPress with access to the underlying file system. This means you will have to install WordPress on your own server or a hosting site that gives you full access to the WordPress file system, such as WPEngine (http://wpengine.com/). If you're using a hosting service (especially a one-click install service like DreamHost), you won't need to worry about most of the details in the following section on installing WordPress, because your hosting service will handle a lot of it, or provide easy-to-use interfaces to walk you through setup.

Installing WordPress

Before installing WordPress on your server, make sure that:

- the server is running PHP version 5.2.4 or greater and MySQL version 5.0 or greater
- you can access the server via shell or FTP
- you have access to and know the URL of the root directory where web files are kept (or a subdirectory within the web root)

- you are able to create a MySQL database and accompanying user on the server

Contact your systems administrator for the above information and access. If you are installing your CBOX site in the same web space as your main website's files, you will want them to create a subdirectory in the root for you. The URL for your CBOX site will then be http:// yoursite.com/subdirectoryname.

To install WordPress, download and unzip the latest version of the software. On your server, create a new MySQL database, and an accompanying user with full access and editing privileges. If you are using a hosting provider, you can contact them or view their documentation to find out about how to create or access your site's database. There may be one already set up for you, or they may have an automated process to guide you through database creation and customization. *Note*: If your hosting provider uses the cPanel hosting control panel, WordPress provides detailed instructions for creating databases and users at http://codex.wordpress.org/Using_cPanel.

The WordPress Codex also gives detailed instructions for using phpMyAdmin, your server's MySQL client, or the DirectAdmin control panel. If you are installing WordPress on a local server, contact your system administrator to find out the best way to access mySQL on your server. If your system administrator creates a database and user for you, make sure to get from them the following information:

- DB_NAME
- DB_USER
- DB_PASSWORD
- DB_HOST

You can now move the unzipped WordPress directory to the desired location on your web server. To run the install script, type your Word-Press URL into your browser. If you put the WordPress directory directly in your site root, the URL will be *http://yoursite.com*, and if you created a subdirectory for it, it will be *http://yoursite.com/subdirectory-name*.

For more detailed instructions, troubleshooting, as well as the latest server requirements for installing WordPress, see http://codex. wordpress.org/Installing_WordPress. For even more detailed instructions on how to install and set up WordPress, along with other library WordPress-based projects and case studies, see the other book in the series, *WordPress for Libraries* by Chad Haefele.

Installing CBOX

When your WordPress site is up and ready to go, log into WordPress at *http://yoursite.com/admin* (or *http://yoursite.com/subdirectoryname/admin*) and in the Plugins section, click *Add New*. Search for "Commons in a Box" and then click the *Install Now* link. (You can also download the plugin directly from http://wordpress.org/plugins/commons-in-a-box/.) If this is the first plugin your install on your new WordPress site, you may need to enter your FTP login credentials, so have them on hand just in case. When the plugin is done installing, click the "Activate Plugin" link to activate it.

Once you've installed the plugin, you will see a prompt to install BuddyPress, which is a set of components for turning WordPress into a social community platform. Click the *Continue* button and WordPress will automatically install all the related plugins needed to turn the site into a CBOX website. When all the plugins have successfully been installed, click on the button that says *Return to the CBOX Dashboard*. The CBOX dashboard provides an easy-to-use control panel for configuring BuddyPress that is broken into four tabs: *Components*, *Pages*, *Permalinks*, and *Finish*. After choosing your desired options on each tab, click the *Save & Next* button in the upper right corner of the dashboard. On the final tab you will click *Finish & Activate* to finalize the process. *Note*: If your existing WordPress theme is not compatible with BuddyPress, you will see a warning and an option to either activate the default CBOX theme, or install a different BuddyPress compatible theme.

Customizing Your Theme

You should now see a CBOX link in the left-hand area of your WordPress admin website. You can use the link to navigate to the CBOX dashboard, where you can configure your Commons site, including changing the theme and managing the plugins you want to use and make available to your community. You can also access your CBOX theme options by clicking on the *Appearance* link in the left-hand menu of your WordPress admin site. This will expand the menu to show all the options under *Appearance*, including *CBOX Theme Options*. Under the "Options" tab you will be able to customize the layout, colors, and fonts on your site, as well as customize the homepage, menus, header, footer, and sidebar areas.

Setting up the Homepage

Many WordPress themes allow you to set up your website to open to an unique page designed specifically to act as a landing page or homepage. The CBOX theme has a default homepage template which is divided into multiple sections, including an image slider and several widget areas, as seen below (see figure 5.8).

You can use the slider to highlight notable groups or posts, community news, events, or new features. The top right widget area is a good place to put account creation/login information. Some other available

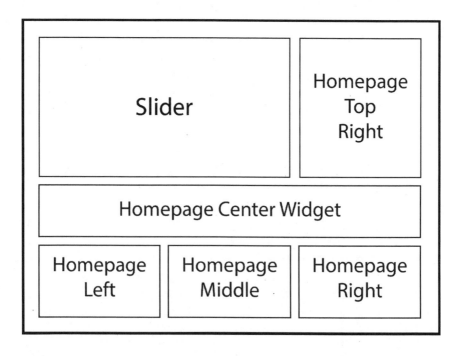

Figure 5.8. CBOX theme default homepage layout

widgets that are often included on the homepage are the *CAC Featured Content* widget, which gives you another spot to feature specific posts or groups, the *Who's Online Avatars* or *Recently Active Members Avatars* widgets, and the *Recently Active Groups* or *Recent Networkwide Blog Posts* widgets. These widgets all allow you to easily and consistently pull recent content to create a dynamic homepage without the need to constantly manually update it. For more information on widgets and how to activate and customize them, see the *Plugins and Widgets* section later in this chapter.

To set up the homepage slider, go to *CBOX Theme Options*, click on *Home Page*, and then click on *Slider Setup*. You will see a drop-down box that gives you the option to either add slides through the *Featured Slider* tool ("Show Site Features"), to add them by automatically pulling all posts labeled with a predefined category tag ("Show Featured Posts from a Category"), or to hide the slider all together ("Do Not Display"). *Note*: Hiding the slider leaves an empty space in its place, which can be fixed by editing the homepage's CSS, via the *Appearance* menu.

If you choose the "Show Site Features" option, you will see a new option under the CBOX menu link called *Featured Slider*. When you click on it, it will open a custom post type designed specifically to display properly in the slider. Give the post a title and some text, and add an image by clicking on the link in the *Featured Image* box to the right of the post. The slide will appear on your homepage when you publish the post.

If you choose the "Show Featured Posts from a Category" option, the slider will automatically pull all posts published within a preset category. (You will still use the *Featured Image* box within the desired posts to add the images.) To set the category, go to *CBOX Theme Options* » *Home Page* » *Featured Slider Category*. Because you can easily switch through slide sets just by changing the featured category, this option is perfect for setting up multiple sets of rotating slides, or if you'd like to rotate through a new set of slides each month and keep the old sets archived under a month/year category. In case you don't want to have to switch out the featured category regularly, you can also set the number of slides you'd like the slider to rotate through, so that the slideshow doesn't keep getting infinitely longer as your site grows.

Some tips for adding images to your slider:

- Images in the slider rotate in order from oldest to newest. To change the order, just edit the publication dates of the posts. (Unpublish or delete a post to remove it from the slider.)
- The slider will scale images down in size, but not up, so be consistent with your image sizes.
- The CBOX documentation site recommends that you use images that are approximately 670 pixels wide × 345 pixels high.
- You can add videos instead of images by clicking on *Video Options* within the post, and then pasting in the YouTube or Vimeo video URL.

Plugins and Widgets

People sometimes confuse the terms *plugin* and *widget* in WordPress-speak. A plugin is tool that you install and activate to add some functionality to WordPress. A widget is a modular unit that can be added to certain areas of your website to display dynamic content or functions. Plugins often have widgets associated with them which allow you to customize how and where the plugin's functionality is displayed. If a plugin includes a widget, it will automatically appear under *Appearance » Widgets*. You can then drag it into one of the available widget areas to activate and customize it. Sometimes there are additional customization options, which you can adjust either in the plugins list, or via the *Settings* link in the left-hand navigation.

You can add and remove plugins through the plugins link in the *Settings* area of the CBOX dashboard, or through the the *Plugins* link in the expanded CBOX menu. There you will find a list of *Recommended Plugins* which are automatically installed and activated when you first set up CBOX. You can deactivate any of the plugins in this list if you choose (however, you cannot uninstall the BuddyPress plugin, which is required for CBOX to function). There is also an *Á la carte!* section, which contains plugins that are not automatically activated because they represent specific functionality that is not always necessary, and/or because they require some extra setup time to configure. All the plugins in both of these lists have been vetted by CBOX developers and are considered safe and compatible with the CBOX and BuddyPress software.

The required BuddyPress plugin adds the following functionality to your WordPress site:

- Site-wide, group, and personal activity streams
- User-created groups
- User-created blogs
- Friend connections
- Extended profiles
- Private messaging
- User settings with customizable notification options

Some other recommended plugins that come preinstalled with CBOX are BuddyPress Docs, which allows users to collaborate on documents (with multiple permission levels and version control); Buddy-Press Docs Wiki, which creates an easily accessible site-wide wiki that all site members can edit; and bbPress, which adds advanced forum functionality to groups. For a more comprehensive list of recommended plugins and their functionality, see http://commonsinabox.org/documentation/plugins.

The BuddyPress and bbPress plugins add site-wide and group functionality, and do not need to be added to any of the widget areas. Plugins that highlight featured content, recent activity, or currently online members usually require that a widget be added to an assigned widget area on one or more of your site's pages. CBOX features multiple widget areas, including the ones in the homepage template, as mentioned in the earlier section on setting up your homepage. There is also an optional site-wide sidebar in which you can place widgets. You can set the sidebar to be located on either the left or the right-hand side of your site via *Appearance » CBOX Theme Options » Options » Sidebar*. Some other areas of your Commons website that have customizable widget areas are the site-wide wiki, members' blogs, group, forum, activity and member pages, and your site's footer, which features three columns in which widgets can be added.

Building Your Community with Groups

Once you've set up your Organizational Commons, it's best to create some spaces for users to interact. Later on, they can start their own groups and blogs, but in the beginning people may just want to get the lay of the land, so give them some blogs to read and some forum posts to get some discussions started. To create a group, click on the *Create a Group* button under the *Groups* tab. You can make the group public, private, or hidden. Users must request membership to join a private group, but it will be listed in the groups' directory. A hidden group is only visible to members, who must be invited to join. You can also choose if you'd like your group to have forums, and an associated blog.

When you are first populating your Commons site, you may want to create a group for each department in your library. Each department can then have a blog where people can post important updates or announcements, and forums where members can raise questions or issues that other members can then respond to. This is a great way to get coworkers interacting and helping each other out, and can save managers the time and frustration of having to answer the same question over and over for different people, or having to settle issues that can be resolved directly among coworkers.

The final step when creating a group allows you to send invites to staff members. You can now easily invite department members to their respective groups and give them a reason to sign up for your exciting new CBOX website.

HOW TO BUILD A LIBRARY INTRANET SITE IN MICROSOFT SHAREPOINT

Did you ever wish you could create your own library website for your staff? Library employees navigate the library web site differently, and need quick access to the most commonly requested links and resources. They also have access to additional tools, documents, and resources which you may not want to make publicly available on your regular website. With Microsoft SharePoint, you can easily create an internal website for the library, with password protection for limited-access resources, customized resource and link lists, and social features. SharePoint lets you bring together important resources like calendars, documents, links, contact information, and news, giving employees access to everything they need through one portal.

There are several options for implementing SharePoint at your institution. If your library is part of a larger entity, like a university or corporation, it may already have SharePoint installed and licensed, so you will be able to create and manage your library site entirely through a web browser without installing any software or having to directly access the server where the software is installed. Contact your information technology (IT) department or systems administrator to find out who manages your SharePoint intranet. You'll need to get the URL of the organization's SharePoint site from them, as well as the instructions for setting up your account with the proper permissions which allows you to create sites within the larger SharePoint site.

SharePoint 2013 also includes a cloud-based option, SharePoint Online, as a part of their Office 365 suite. You will not need to install anything or set anything up on your local server to use this version. SharePoint standalone (which does not include any of the other Office 365 products, like Microsoft Word, Excel, or PowerPoint) costs a minimum of $3 per user per month, so you will need to budget for about $200 per year for a very small staff, or $900 per year for a staff of twenty-five. *Note*: There is also a free, limited-feature version of SharePoint that you can run on your own Windows server, called SharePoint Foundation. If you're interested in running SharePoint on your own server, you can download the free version at http://www.microsoft.com/download/details.aspx?id=35488. For in-depth installation instructions, see Microsoft's free e-book, *Deployment Guide for SharePoint 2013*, which is available in a variety of formats for download at http://www.microsoft.com/download/details.aspx?id=30384.

Creating a Library Portal in SharePoint

When you are ready to set up a SharePoint site for your library, navigate to your institution's SharePoint URL in a web browser, and sign in with the username and password assigned by your SharePoint administrator. If you decide to use SharePoint Online, you will first have to create a Microsoft Office 365 account at http://portal.office.com. Once logged in, you'll see a link called *Sites* in the bar at the top of the page. This is how you will access your SharePoint sites.

If you have set up your own installation for the library, or if you are using SharePoint Online, you can set up your main library portal by clicking on the Team Site block. Later, if you decide to create additional sites to act as portals for specific departments, you can add them as subsites. This way, you can have a generic library portal, as well as customized portals for reference staff, circulation staff, interlibrary loan, and so forth.

If you are using your organization's SharePoint installation to house your library portal, you can create a subsite in that system by clicking on the gear icon in the upper right-hand corner of the page, and selecting *Site contents* from the drop-down list. Under the *Site Contents* section you should see a section called *Subsites*, with a link to create a new subsite. A subsite can *also* have subsites, so even if your library portal is a subsite of a larger system, you can still create additional subsites within it for library departments.

When creating a site, you'll be given the option to choose a URL. The main team site for your SharePoint intranet is the URL you or your organization chose when setting up SharePoint, for example, www.myuniversityportal.com or www.mylibraryportal.com. Subsites take the main site's URL and append it with a slash and a title, like a directory system on a server. So if you create a library subsite in your university's system, for example, it will look like this: www.myuniversityportal.com/library, and if you create departmental subsites they will look like this: www.myuniversityportal.com/library/reference. You can change both the title and the URL of a site after it is created by clicking on *Site Contents* » *Settings* » *Title, description, and logo*. Keep in mind that these are the URLs your staff will use to access the appropriate portal, so keep them short, descriptive, and avoid spaces or special characters.

When creating new sites, you will be asked to choose a site template. The site template determines the general structure of that site, along with what apps, web parts (which will be covered later in this section), and the default navigation that your site will include. The basic options for templates include:

- *team site*: a collaborative workspace;
- *blog*: limited-function site used mainly for posting and commenting on updates and ideas;
- *project site*: basically a team site but designed to focus on a specific project; and

- *community site*: a social site that focuses on discussion and inter-action.

When in doubt, it's usually best to choose the team site template which includes an array of useful functions and is the most flexible of the templates. You can always add blogs, project sites, and community sites as subsites within your team site if you want to give people the opportunity to start an internal blog or if you want to give people a space to work on a specific project. Community sites are built strictly to encourage communication and interaction among users and are not good for enabling document or calendar sharing, so they should be limited to uses such as book groups or discussion lists that require a moderator.

Setting User Permissions

As discussed in previous chapters, *Permissions* are the set of actions a user can perform within a website or application. In SharePoint, the user only sees the options for actions they are granted permissions for. So if a user is not allowed to edit a page in your site, they will not see that option. Permissions in SharePoint can get pretty granular since you can set them for sites, applications, and even specific files. When you create a new site, you will be asked to set the permissions for the site.

The default setting for subsites is to share the permissions of their parent site, so if you want to create a subsite that is visible and/or editable by a specific group of staff members (for a department in the library, for example), you must toggle to *Use unique permissions* under *User Permissions.* This is particularly important if you plan on assigning an administrator to a departmental subsite who is not an administrator on the main site. Permissions can always be edited later, but if you originally set the permissions to *Use same permissions*, any future administrator of that subsite will also need to be assigned as an administrator of the parent site in order to edit the subsite's permissions.

If you do choose to assign unique permissions, you will be given the option to create groups with specific permissions within the site (or, if you've already created some sites, you can reuse the groups from those). Later, when you start adding users to your system, you can put those users in groups to determine what sites they have access to. The

SharePoint team site template automatically creates the following groups with the associated permission levels:

- *Visitors*: are able to view content
- *Members*: are able to view and to contribute content
- *Owners*: are able to view and contribute content, and have access to site or app settings

The full list of permission levels that can be granted to users or groups include:

- *Limited Access*: users can view specific lists, document libraries, list items, folders, or documents when given permissions
- *View Only*: users can view pages, list items, and documents
- *Read*: users can view pages and list items and download documents
- *Contribute*: users can view, add, update, and delete list items and documents
- *Edit*: users can add, edit, and delete lists; can view, add, update, and delete list items and documents
- *Design*: users can view, add, update, delete, approve, and customize
- *Full Control*: users have full control over content and settings
- *Create new subsites*: users can create new subsites

Note: If you are a site administrator, you can also create custom permission levels, each with a specific set of permitted actions for a user or group. (Remember when I said that permissions in SharePoint can get pretty granular?) For the complete list of user permissions and permission levels, see http://technet.microsoft.com/library/cc721640.aspx.

Keep in mind that any documents or applications that are added to a site will initially share the same permissions as their parent, so subsites, lists, and libraries inherit the permissions of their parent site, folders inherit the permissions of the list or library that contains them, and list items or documents inherit the permissions of the folder that contains them. To create a unique set of permissions for an item, select it and click *Manage » Shared With » ADVANCED* to open the file's permissions tab. Then click on *Stop Inheriting Permissions* at the top of the page. You can now choose what individual users or groups of users can view, edit, or manage the item.

Setting Up the Home Page

When you have created your new SharePoint site (or, if this is a brand new account or installation, when you've clicked on the Team Site tile to open your main site), you will see a default homepage with many areas that you can customize (see figure 5.9). There are some tiles with suggested actions on them to get you started. For now, you can click on the link to remove them (instructions for adding these elements will be covered later in this section).

If you click on the PAGE tab in the top left corner and then click Edit, you can add some text to your homepage, like a welcome message, or some initial instructions to users. There is also a navigational menu along the left side of the page called the Quick Launch. You can edit this navigation as you like, including adding links to websites and files outside of SharePoint. Many of the links from within SharePoint can just be dragged and dropped into the Quick Launch when you click on *Edit Links*. Some useful links to add to this menu are Site Pages, which will list all the pages you've created for the site, Site Assets, which lists any image, audio, or video files added to the site, and Site Settings, where you configure settings such as user permissions, site metadata, and site design options. Site Pages and Site Assets can be added to the

Figure 5.9. Microsoft SharePoint site-builder dashboard

navigation by clicking on Site Contents in the Quick Launch, then click-ing Edit Links, and then clicking on and dragging the desired tile from the main content section of the page, and dropping it into the Quick Launch section. When you're in edit mode, you can also reorder the links, or next one link under another. The Site Settings link cannot be dragged and dropped, so you can right click on it to save the link location, and then add it manually by clicking the add link button. (This is also how you add external links to your navigation.)

There is another navigation section at the top of the page which you edit in the same way as the Quick Launch. After you've created some pages and used your site for a while, it will become clear what parts or your site, or perhaps subsites, you'd like quick and easy access to. Your users may also request that you add certain links or that you move them from one menu to the other. Just don't change them around too much or too often or you'll confuse your users!

Adding Web Parts to your SharePoint Intranet Site

The key to creating a successful intranet site for your library is to make it useful. (Duh.) Don't just mimic your regular website or another read-ily available resource. Bring together resources that are normally spread out in different places, that people may have saved locally or have in print, but are not currently available over the Internet. You can use Web Parts in SharePoint to easily create shared calendars, a document library, contact information, resource lists, and announcements (see figure 5.10). This section will discuss how to add a calendar, announce-ment, issue tracking, and knowledge base Web Part to your SharePoint homepage so users will see those items as soon as they log in.

One of the most useful Web Parts you can add to your site, and especially to your homepage, is calendars. SharePoint comes prein-stalled with a calendar app which lets you create multiple calendars in the system and to merge selected calendars so they can be viewed together. To create a new calendar, go to the Site Contents page and click *add an app*. (You can also add apps via the gear icon in the top right corner of the website.) Choose Calendar from the list of available apps, and give your calendar a name. Once it's been created, you will see your new calendar listed on your Site Contents Page. To add a calendar to your site's homepage, click the Home link in the Quick

Launch, and then click on the Page tab to open the page editing options. Now click *Edit* in the ribbon at the top of the page, and then click the *Insert* tab. Choose Web Part from the ribbon of available options, choose the calendar you'd like to add to the page, and click the *add* button in the bottom right corner of the pane.

Figure 5.10. Sample SharePoint Homepage with Announcements, Document Library, Contacts, and Calendar Web Parts

Since you will want to add multiple Web Parts to the homepage, you probably don't want the calendar to display as large as it does by default. When you scroll your cursor over the top right corner of the pane, a small triangle will appear, indicating a drop-down list. Click on the triangle and select *Edit Web Part* from the list. You can customize the size of the calendar by expanding the *Appearance* section, where you can specify the desired height and width in pixels. 500 × 500 pixels will allow you to see a smaller version of the calendar without adding scrollbars. You can also choose to display upcoming events from the calendar instead of the calendar itself by changing the *Selected View* from *Calendar* to *All Events* or *Current Events*. When you are done customizing your calendar, click OK, and then remember to click on the Save button at the top of the page so you don't lose your page edits.

You can also create multiple calendars and display a master calendar on the homepage which merges them. First, create the calendars by adding them as apps on the Site Content page. Then create a new master calendar and open it. Open the calendar's editing ribbon by clicking the *Calendar* tab, and then click *Calendars Overlay*. To add another calendar, click *New Calendar*, and give the calendar you are adding a name. (This may seem confusing, since you want to add a calendar that already exists, and this makes it look like you are creating a new calendar. What you are actually doing though, is creating and naming an *overlay*, where another calendar's information will be overlaid on top of this calendar.) Under *Web URL*, make sure your Share-Point site URL is correctly displayed, and click *Resolve*. You should now see a drop-down list of available calendars to add to the current one. Once you've created a master calendar, you can add it to your homepage via the method described above.

Another useful item to include on your homepage is an announcements section so users can see what's new as soon as they log in. You will create your announcements Web Part in the same way you did your calendar, by adding it as an app from the Site Contents page, or by clicking on the gear icon and selecting *Add an app*. Now go back to your homepage and click *Page » Edit » Insert » Web Part*. Choose *Announcements* from the available apps, and then click the *Add* button. Remember to click *Save* at the top of the page before adding any announcements, or you will have to start over.

To make your announcements display alongside your calendar instead of under it, go back to *Page » Edit*, and change the Text Layout to *Two columns* (or whatever your desired layout is). You can also change the height and width of the announcements section in the same way you did for your calendar, as well as choose if you'd like just the title of the announcement or an announcement summary to display.

You may also want to include an area on your homepage for contact information for staff members. SharePoint includes a Contacts app, which you activate as previously described. Once you've added it to the homepage (*Page » Edit » Insert » Web Part*), you can move it to the opposite column by dragging and dropping it to the desired location on the page.

Some other useful Web Parts you may want to add to your homepage, or just to your site, are the Issue Tracking app, Link Lists, Task Lists, and Surveys. *Note*: A Document Library Web Part is automatically added to your homepage when you create a new site, but you can also add apps for a Picture Library, Form Library, Asset Library, and Report Library.

Adding Web Parts increases the functionality of your site, but you may not want to include all of them on your homepage, or it will appear cluttered and confusing to users. Once you've added a Web Part, it will then be included on the Site Contents page, where you can drag it and drop it into your Quick Launch menu (when in edit mode), so users can easily find Web Parts that are not listed on the homepage.

Working with Document Libraries

One of the most useful and utilized parts of Microsoft SharePoint is its document library feature. Document libraries are actually Web Parts which can be added as apps, but every new site that you create will already have a document library by default. You can set the permission levels of individual documents to control who can view, edit, and download them, or you can create document libraries for specific projects or departments, and set the permissions at the library level.

Document libraries are an asset to SharePoint for several reasons. They give you a central location to store documents which does not require its own server space, for which users would need FTP access or the ability to map a drive on their computer. Because SharePoint is accessible over the Internet (as well as via mobile apps), users can access and work on their documents from anywhere. As with the other knowledge bases mentioned in this chapter, SharePoint document libraries provide version control and a revision history for each document, with an added "check out" feature. When a document is checked out by one user, it is locked and cannot be edited by other users. They will see a little green box with an arrow next to the document indicating that it is currently unavailable. If they scroll over the green box, they can also see the name of the user who has checked the document out. When you are done editing, you must check the document back in to open it back up to editing by others. The resulting dialog box will also give you an area to leave comments about your edits.

In SharePoint Online, you will likely have to enable *Version History* for each document library you create in order to view previous versions of documents in those libraries. To enable this feature, open the desired document library, click on the *Library* tab at the top of the page, and then click on *Library Settings*. Under *General Settings*, choose *Versioning Settings*. In this section you can enable content approval as well as enable versioning. You can also decide if you want to save only versions of the file where major changes were made, or if you'd like to save a greater number of draft revisions. You can also limit the number of versions saved in the system. This can be important if you are using SharePoint on your own server and have limited server space. Finally, you can require that users check out a document to edit it.

To create a new document or folder in a document library, click on *new* at the top of the document list. You can also upload documents into the library from your computer. To move a file into a folder, click on the *Library* tab and in the *Connect & Export* section, select *Open with Explorer*. This will open a Windows Explorer window, inside which you can drag and drop files into or out of folders. *Note*: This function may not work on browsers other than Internet Explorer. If the option is not available, you can send a copy of the file to the folder by following these steps:

- Right-click the destination folder to copy the link location.
- Click the shaded box at the front of the document you want to move to select it (a checkmark will appear).
- Open the *Files* tab and click *Send To » Other Destination* in the *Copies* section.
- Paste the URL and click OK.
- Delete the original file if you don't need copies in both locations (because you actually created a new copy of the file in the folder, rather than actually moving it).

Creating a Knowledge Base in SharePoint

One of the benefits of having an organizational intranet is that it helps connect staff members who don't regularly work closely together and enables them to share and store information in a central location. SharePoint allows you to add a wiki to your site, which you can use to create a shared knowledge base. Your staff can use the wiki to collect common reference questions and to collaborate on their answers, to create custom lists of references and links pertinent to specific groups of users, or to create internal pages for book groups, storytimes, or other events. Wikis are also great for documentation, instructions, or for creating online training manuals.

The default wiki page library can be found under the Site Pages link in SharePoint, which can be found under Site Content (if you did not already add the Site Pages link to your Quick Launch, as recommended earlier in this section). SharePoint automatically includes a wiki page called "How to Use This Library," which goes over the basics of creating and editing pages, adding links, viewing a page's revision history, and managing the wiki page library. You can create multiple wiki page libraries, so it's best to leave the Site Pages one for the main pages of your intranet. Think carefully about what wikis you'd like to have ahead of time so you can create a separate library for each (i.e., Training Materials, Reference Questions, Events, etc.). This way, you can set the permissions for each wiki to restrict who can edit and view those pages. To create a new wiki, simply add it as a new Wiki Page Library app via the *Your Apps* page, and give it a unique, descriptive name.

The key to creating and maintaining a successful library intranet site in SharePoint is to make it as convenient and easy to use as possible. Take your time in both the planning and training stages, to make sure you're meeting actual needs and not just creating another site for your staff to check. Gather feedback early and often to see how you can make it work for your users. SharePoint is a very robust system and can do many things, which can quickly lead to you and your users being overwhelmed, so define the key tasks you'd like people to be able to accomplish through the library portal, and don't over complicate things with too many features or functions. For an in-depth look at SharePoint setup, customization, and features, see *Microsoft SharePoint 2013 Step by Step* by Olga M. Londer and Penelope Coventry.

HOW TO CREATE A DYNAMIC FAQ WITH SPRINGSHARE'S LIBANSWERS

A well-designed, well-maintained frequently asked questions (FAQ) document can be invaluable to both patrons and staff alike. But a FAQ is only useful if users can find the question–answer pair which gives them the information they need. Librarians can often predict what questions patrons are most likely to ask based on the questions they most often receive at the library's reference desk, but the LibAnswers system from Springshare helps librarians build the knowledge base in a number of other ways. For example, you can not only add your own questions based on your knowledge and experience helping patrons, but you can also use the software's QuerySpy tool to check what questions and keywords users are searching for, even if they don't click on any of the results or submit a question to the system. QuerySpy can clue you in to how users are choosing to word their questions, what keywords they're using, and what they're clicking on (if they click on anything) in relation to what they type in the search box. You can also choose to include user-submitted questions in the FAQ with just a few clicks!

Before you start adding entries to your FAQ, there are some administrative things you will need to take care of. In fact, adding question-and-answer pairs is probably one of the last things you'll do before launch. This project is broken down into the following tasks:

- System setup
- System settings
- Setting up your queue(s)
- Setting up LibChat
- Creating datasets for reference analytics
- Creating groups
- Creating accounts/adding users
- Adding FAQ entries
- Creating widgets
- Answering questions

Getting Started: System Setup

Once you sign into your LibAnswers site, you will see an orange menu bar at the top of the page. Under the Admin drop-down, select *System Settings* (see figure 5.11). Here you will be able to set some basic administrative options for the system.

First, you can choose a name for your system, like "Ask a Librarian" or "Library FAQ." You will also want to add an administrative contact e-mail address. This person is the main administrative contact for the system, and will also be copied on the e-mail whenever someone submits a tech support issue through the link at the bottom of every patron-facing page. Next make sure to include the URL and name of your library, so that LibAnswers can link users back to your library's main website through their breadcrumb navigation. If you are part of a library system that includes other libraries using LibAnswers, you can

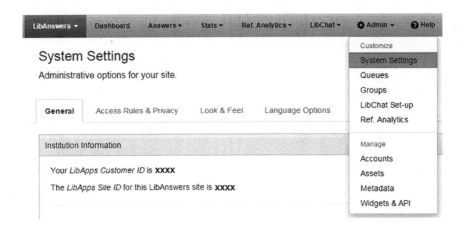

Figure 5.11. LibAnswers Admin Menu and System Settings

link to their systems via the "Related Systems" section, using their iid(s), or site identifier(s). These are unique numbers assigned to each Lib-Guides, LibAnswers, LibCal, or other Springshare system, and can be found at the end of the URL of the admin sign-in screen. (To find the iid for a LibAnswers site, go to that site's login page, look at the URL, and copy the number after "iid=." Separate multiple iids with commas.) The next option is to set your time zone. This is particularly important because it will not only affect timestamps on incoming questions, but also be used to trigger offline messages for your chat reference service.

The rest of the page contains optional settings, including an additional support URL or e-mail (if you'd like the support e-mails to go to someone other than the administrative contact, or if you'd like to redirect to a separate ticketing or IT help system), and a place to add helpful links like the library's online catalog, popular databases, or other useful resources. You can also customize the results page, add your local IP range to identify on-campus users, and add tracking codes from popular website statistics services like Google Analytics.

If you'd like to customize your LibAnswers site to look more like your library's website or your LibGuides, you can upload a banner image, insert custom CSS or JavaScript, or change the site's colors via the "Look & Feel" tab. The final tab in *System Settings* is the "Admin Alert Box," which lets you include a message or announcement which all administrative users will see when they first log into the system. This is a great way to introduce users to new or highlighted features, system downtime, or even just provide positive feedback, especially when you are first launching your system.

When a user submits a question into the LibAnswers system, it is called a ticket. Tickets are routed into a queue where staff can claim them and respond. Only one queue is included in the system by default, but you can add additional queues (one for each department, for example) for an extra fee. Each queue comes with its own e-mail address, SMS number, and Twitter handle. Because of the extra cost associated with adding additional queues, this project will assume the library is using only one queue to handle all incoming tickets. If you decided to add queues to your subscription (for different departments, or to create separate queues for internal and external users, for example) you can set them up in the same manner as outlined below.

To set up your queue, click the Admin dropdown and select *Queues*. Under the "Question Form" tab, you can customize the form that patrons will use to submit tickets to the system. Under *General Settings*, compose the text you'd like users to see at the top of the form. This can be instructions, like "please include your e-mail address" or it can include helpful information like estimated response times. Next, under *Success Message*, you can customize the text you'd like users to see upon submitting the form. In this section you can also include your business hours, and set an alternate message to be displayed during your off-hours.

The next section, *Form Fields*, is very important because it controls what information is recorded into your statistics, so think carefully about what information you want to gather from your patrons. You can add a maximum of three multiple choice and three free text fields to your question form. There is also an optional *Question Routing Field* available. You can use this section to allow the user to select a category or topic for their question, and then control where the question is routed based on their answer. If you have multiple queues, you can use this field to direct departmental questions to the appropriate department or person. Or, alternatively, if every department in your library has its own departmental e-mail account, you can assign questions to those accounts based on the user's selection. (This may require creating a separate LibAnswers account for each department, as well as each user, as questions can only be routed to a queue or a user, not a group or group of users.)

In the next set of tabs you can set up your system e-mail preferences and templates. Make sure to use the *Test E-mail Settings* box to check your settings and confirm that your e-mail is working, and that you are happy with the layout, appearance, and content of the e-mail notifications. Under the Notifications tab you can include any e-mail addresses of users who you'd like to receive a notification from every time someone submits a ticket to the system. You can add as many e-mail addresses as you like, but if you are forwarding e-mails from a generic library or reference account into the system, make sure you *do not* include that e-mail address in the notifications field.

Next you can set up your Twitter and SMS messaging. Just add your library's Twitter handle into the system, and any messages sent to that account will automatically be forwarded into the system. You can also replay directly from the system to both Twitter and SMS, so no need to log into multiple accounts to field incoming questions!

Also included with LibAnswers is LibChat, a chat reference service. You can set up your chat service by clicking on *LibChat Set Up*, which is also located in the Admin drop-down. In this section you are able to create separate chat accounts for each library department, add users to those department accounts, craft preset messages for quick and easy responses to commonly asked questions, and build chat widgets to embed on your website, catalog, or other online library resource.

The final step in the system setup process is deciding what data you want to track if you're planning on using LibAnswers to collect statistics and generate reports. These are essentially the set of questions that staff will use to describe each patron interaction, including tickets that come in via Twitter, SMS, LibChat, or questions forms. Because different departments might want to collect different information from users, you can create a separate set of questions for each department. The system refers to each of these sets of questions as datasets, and you should think carefully about what kind of reports you want to generate, because changing these datasets later will result in inconsistent reporting and make it difficult to compare current reports to past statistics. If you want to be able to compare your statistics directly with past reports from before using LibAnswers, you should make sure to break transactions down in the same way you did in the past. Going forward, you can always add additional questions or options without compromising the integrity of your data.

The newest version of LibAnswers gives you the option to create groups, which you can use to organize your knowledge base into sections, each with its own set of FAQs and user access levels. Some examples of times you would want to use groups in your system are:

- You'd like staff members to only be able to add and edit content within their own departments, so you would create a group for each department.
- You want to separate your system into a public knowledge base with FAQs for patrons, and an internal one with FAQs for staff.
- You want to create a small knowledge base for a special project or committee, accessible only to specific users who have been invited.

Click on *Groups* under the Admin menu to create or edit groups. Here you can set the group as publicly available, viewable only to those logged into the system, or viewable to only those with invited access (you can invite people via the *User Access* tab). *Note*: System admins have universal access to all groups and queues, even if you set them as restricted. Keep this in mind when setting the user permission levels of new accounts, which is covered in the following section.

Creating Accounts/Adding Users

Once you've set up your LibAnswers system, you're ready to start adding user accounts for staff who will be answering tickets and adding FAQs. Under the Admin drop-down, select *Accounts*. Enter the user's e-mail address under the *Create a New Account* tab. If your library is already using LibGuides and the user has an account there, the system will be able to pull information to prepopulate many of the form fields. When adding a user to LibAnswers, you must set their access levels. The overall access you want to give the user to the system is set in the *User Level* field. The following are the available levels of access and their associated privileges:

- Admin:

–Claim, answer, create, edit, and transfer tickets

–Manage Reference Analytics transactions and view all system statistics

–Add, edit, and delete FAQs

–Add, edit, and delete accounts

–Customize the look & feel of the system

–Create and edit widgets

–Change e-mail notification and social media settings

–Restrict access to the system

- Regular:

  –Claim, answer, create, edit, and transfer tickets

  –Add and edit Reference Analytics transactions and view general statistics

  –Create widgets

  –Edit personal LibAnswers account

- Reader:

  –Can access LibAnswers system even if password protected or otherwise restricted

- Ref. Analytics Only:

  –Can enter statistics, but not access queues or FAQs

You also have the option to set a user as inactive, which allows you to remove their access to the system without removing their statistics. (You will only see this option once an account has been created and you go back in to edit it.) After setting a user's overall access level, you can also then give them additional access privileges or restrict their access privileges to specific queues and groups. In this way you can make a regular user an admin in a specific queue or group, or you can restrict a regular user's access to a specific queue or group. Be careful giving users full Admin permissions, because as mentioned in the last section, they will automatically have access to all groups and queues. *Tip*: If you want to create a group that a system admin should not have access to, you can demote that user on the system level to a regular user, and then give them admin access to all the groups and queues except the restricted one.

When creating user accounts, you can also select the default analytics dataset for that user, or the set of reference analytics questions that they will see by default whenever they enter a transaction into the system. Users can choose to switch to a different dataset on a transaction-by-transaction basis. You can also assign the user to their respective department(s) to control what tickets they are responsible for fielding via LibChat.

Adding FAQ entries

With all the administrative settings configured, and your system populated with users to help you with the task, you can now start adding content to your LibAnswers knowledge base. To add a question/answer pair, click on the Answers drop down to expand it, and then click *Create FAQ Entry* (see figure 5.12). If you are using groups in your system, first select the group knowledge base you'd like to add the FAQ to, and then type in the question and click the button to continue to the answer screen. When answering the question, you can also embed images (such as screenshots), attach files (like any relevant forms), or include media (like video tutorials). You can also add links to related content or resources, and assign topics and keywords to make the FAQ findable in any of the various ways your users may search for it.

Some tips for creating good FAQs include:

- Ask around the library and collect a list of the most commonly asked questions. They usually deal with things like hours, general policies for using the building and materials, technology, and directions. Start building your system with these questions, and work your way to the more specific topics.
- When composing questions, choose casual wording and avoid jargon. How would an actual user ask the question? That's the language you want to use.
- When composing answers, be concise and avoid large blocks of text. Break text up into bulleted lists or with images. Whenever referring to online content, including related FAQs, LibGuides, or databases, provide a link so users can easily find and access what you're talking about.

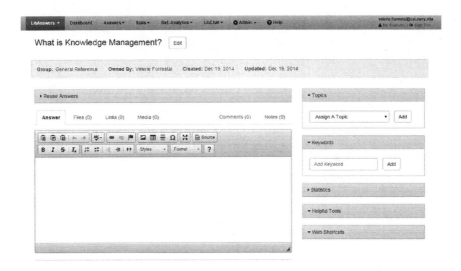

Figure 5.12. Edit FAQ entry/compose answer screen

- Be consistent with your formatting. Don't change fonts or font sizes. Use bold, italics, and colors sparingly. If you are copying and pasting content from other sources, use the "Paste as plain text" button (located right next to the regular paste button in the inline text editor) to remove any formatting from your text, so it will match whatever destination formatting styles you have set.
- "Topics" allow users to browse the knowledge base by category, so think about the ways in which a user might want to browse content. You can create new topics as you add them, and you can add multiple topics to one FAQ. Some examples of good topics include:

  - Audience (e.g. "for students," "for faculty," "for alumni," etc.)
  - Material type (e.g. "books," "newspapers," "DVDs," etc.)
  - Type of help needed (e.g. "tech problems," "citation help," etc.)
  - Associated library or school department, subject area, or course information

- "Keywords" is a more free-form way of adding metadata to your FAQs. Since you browse the system by Topics, you need to keep a fairly regulated list of available topics to use, since browsing a long list becomes cumbersome and confusing. Keywords, on the other hand, don't appear in the patron's view of the answer, so you can add as many as you like. Keywords should be words that are not included in the actual question, but that represent alternative phraseology that patrons may use, including synonyms, colloquialisms, abbreviations, acronyms, and nicknames.

Creating Widgets

LibAnswers widgets allow you to create "portable content," so you can take pieces of your knowledge base and embed them in other locations like your library website, LibGuides, the library catalog or databases, or a course management system like Blackboard or Moodle. You can find the widget creation tool under the Admin menu. The types of widgets you can build are:

- *Search Form*: A simple search box that allows users to search the knowledge base. *Note*: search can be restricted to specific groups.
- *Question Form*: A form that allows users to submit a question to the system. *Note*: if you have multiple queues, each widget must specify which queue to direct questions that come in through that particular widget.
- *Topic List*: Displays available topics in a group in list, cloud, or drop-down format. You can specify the number of topics to show, which can be sorted alphabetically or by number of FAQs tagged with that topic.
- *FAQ List*: Displays a predefined set of FAQs. You can choose to display a list of recent, popular, topic-specific, custom chosen FAQs, or a single FAQ entry. This is a great option for widgets embedded in LibGuides, since you can choose questions of particular relevance to a specific course, project, or subject area, and just display those. This option also works well for widgets embedded alongside tools or services, since you can select FAQs that address using that tool or service, right at the point of need.
- *Chat widgets*: Create and manage chat widgets via *Admin » LibChat Set Up » System Chat Widgets*. Simple click-to-build interface. View previews of the widget you're building in real time underneath the widget-builder.

Answering Questions

Ideally many users will be able to find the information they need already in your LibAnswers system, but in the case that they cannot find what they need, they can also submit a question through e-mail, question forms, SMS, Twitter, or LibChat. These questions get listed in your queue, and are referred to as tickets. When a ticket comes into the queue, click on it to claim it. This will let other librarians know that someone is working on it so multiple people don't try to answer the same question. If you claim a question by mistake, you can always unclaim it or transfer it to another librarian from the answer page.

Before answering a new question, you can use the search form located in the "Helpful Tools" box on the right of the screen to search the system for similar FAQs, so you don't have to start from scratch if a similar answer already exists. You can also add links to useful resources or attach files that might be helpful to the patron. Finally, you can select whether or not you want to add this question into the general knowledge base (tickets are private; only those logged into the system can view them). If the question is novel and you think it will be useful for other patrons, add it to the appropriate FAQ group. Don't worry, you'll be given a chance to edit the question and answer in the next step, and all patron information will be removed.

This project outlines the major steps in setting up and launching your LibAnswer system, but you can find more detailed setup information in Springshare's own knowledge base of documentation and help materials (you know they had to have one, they're in the knowledge base game!) at http://support.springshare.com/libanswers.

It's almost time to get started on a project of your own, but before you do, make sure to check out the next chapter with helpful project management and technology implementation tips and tricks so you can launch your new system like a pro!

6

TIPS AND TRICKS

Sometimes the hardest part of implementing a new tool in your library is not setting up the software, but instead convincing managers and administrators to support the project, getting staff to try the new system out, and finding ways to *keep* them using it. The three most important factors in making your project a success are:

1. Planning, planning, planning! Do your homework so you can choose the best tool for the job and for your library. Find some key players who have the power, experience, and/or enthusiasm to help you gain buy-in from the rest of the staff.
2. Build the best system for your library's needs. Make it easy on your (potential) users, or they simply won't use it. Don't give them any excuse to avoid using the system. Anticipate problems and questions wherever possible, and have training and help materials at the ready. Make the transition from old workflows to new workflows as seamless as possible.
3. Keep the ball rolling. Old habits die hard, and while you may convince staff to try out the new system, it will be easy for them to fall back into their old ways of doing things. Provide regular reminders and rewards for your users. Stay active with the system and don't let the content stagnate.

Let's look at each of these in a little bit more detail, so you can make sure that all of your hard work results in a successful project implementation.

PLANNING, PLANNING, PLANNING!

You don't have to be a project management expert to implement some basic project management strategies in the planning stages of your knowledge base implementation. Make a list of the major tasks that should be done before, during, and after the launch, include estimates of how long each task will take, and which tasks can be done concurrently. For example, two tasks that should be done during the actual implementation phase of your project are to prepopulate the knowledge base with existing documentation and to prepare training materials to make available to staff after launch. If you do these tasks concurrently, you can use your own experiences as a new user to help you formulate and select training materials because you will encounter some of the same problems, issues, or questions that your users will when they begin using the system.

Now is also the best time to think about the scope and possible scaling of your system because it may affect how you structure the content at the beginning. If you are developing the system for a particular department, can other departments easily be added later? If you are developing it for the whole library, is there a way to give each department their own space if they want one? What will the costs be if you decide that you need more storage space or more user accounts? Will it be reasonable for student workers or volunteers to be trained on the system? Having the answers to these questions sooner rather than later will save you headaches later on.

It's also very important not to develop your system in a vacuum. Let people know what you are working on! This will give you a chance to talk to users and find out what the weaknesses and strengths of the current system are. Your new system has a much better chance of success if it makes people's lives easier, either by adding desired functionality, or by streamlining workflows, but you'll only know what staff wants if you ask them. This also gives you an excellent opportunity to build hype and to find some potential allies for your project who you can tap for not only support when pushing the project through, but for valuable feedback and insights. These "super-users" will also be more equipped to answer questions and provide extra help should they witness someone having trouble with the system.

BUILDING THE BEST SYSTEM

Chapter 3 talked about the plethora of knowledge management systems available, along with their strengths and weaknesses. But building the best knowledge management system for your library entails more than just choosing the best tool for the job. Once you've selected the software you want to use, you need to think about how your colleagues will be using the tool. The easier and more appealing you make the new system, the more likely people will be to actually use it. Here are some tips for building a user-friendly knowledge base:

- Pre-populate, but weed: Migrating content from one system to another is a great time to go over your content for accuracy, timeliness and redundancy. Get rid of or rework anything that's old and out-of-date, or that lacks clarity or function. Do make sure, however, that there's enough content in the new system that users are not faced with blank pages when they first sign in. It's important that they can see a clear focus and purpose for the knowledge base right from the start, or they may not log in a second time!
- Do some of the work for them: If possible, create their accounts in advance, rather than making them create them themselves. Pre-set common preferences like themes and notifications. Install any plug-ins or add-ons that make the tool easier to use, like more user-friendly text editors or tools that let them import their content from another system.
- Tell them about it: If there are features you want people to use or that you think will make them more likely to use the system, don't just assume they'll find them on their own. Let them know if they can sign into the system using their credentials from another account, or if there are special sharing or linking tools. If it's important that they fill out certain fields in their profile, make sure they know that.
- Create ground rules: You don't need to go all out writing best practices documents (because chances are no one will read them if they're twenty pages long), but you should outline some basic guidelines defining the purpose and scope of the knowledge base and how people should use it. This can include formatting rules, appropriate content suggestions, copyright or sharing restrictions,

and links to examples or other resources when necessary. Because you've already prepopulated the system with some content, your users will already have a basic idea of how everything should work, but it doesn't hurt to put some protocols in writing just in case.

- Get them there: You want to make the transition from users' old workflows to the new system as smooth as possible. Update links on existing resources or shared computers so they can access the new system in the same way they accessed the one it is replacing. Create easy-to-find shortcuts on the desktops and in all the browsers on shared work stations. Think of all of the possible ways users might want to browse or search content in the new system, and facilitate those information seeking behaviors. (For example, build a table of contents, index, and/or menu(s) which helps them scan and locate content easily.) If there are rules for how to link to specific pages or files in the system, make sure to provide visual cues like buttons or icons to induce them to use those to generate links, rather than just copying and pasting the URL from the browser. Keep in mind that users may be coming into the system via these links or alternative entry points when building universal navigation. Make sure that even if they don't enter the system from the home page, they can still navigate around, or at least make sure there's a clearly visible link to the home or entry page.

- Don't leave them stranded: Provide training materials in various formats, such as text, screenshots, video tutorials, and so forth. People have different learning styles and you will avoid frustration and make your users very happy if they can choose the help format that best suits their needs. Most popular software tools have their own rich online help documentation, so comb through those websites and curate a list of the best resources for your users. If your institution also uses whatever software system you are implementing, see if they have any resources or workshop you can make available to your staff. Make sure that the "help" link is visible on all pages/sites in the system, and where possible, add point-of-need guidance like "what's this?" links or "more information" pop-ups or buttons. Finally, provide users with a place to go with questions, comments, or problems. Ideally, you can include this information in the footer of every page, but if that is not possible, it should at least be clearly identifiable in all help documentation.

KEEP THE BALL ROLLING

After launch, you want to make sure that people not only try the new system out, but continue to use it into the future. With this purpose in mind, keeping the content fresh and up-to-date is of the utmost importance. If users notice that information is not being updated on a regular basis, or that most of their coworkers have stopped signing in and/or interacting in the system, they will most likely stop using it themselves. To keep yourself from getting overwhelmed with the responsibility of monitoring all content and making most of the updates, you should assign key personnel to update information for their department, committee, working group, or project. You may still have to prompt them occasionally, but it will help that they know that the responsibility for that section of the knowledge base lies with them.

Also, just because you've launched doesn't mean you should stop soliciting feedback. Make sure there is a visible link or form for users to submits their comments, and actively solicit feedback in meetings and by e-mail. User testing should be done on a regular basis, even if informal or on a small scale.

Create incentive programs to showcase and reward staff members who actively or innovatively use the system. Many websites are beginning to include digital badges or digital badge add-ons that allow users to "unlock" and highlight achievements within the system. You can also commend these "high achievers" in monthly e-mails or meetings, and reward them with a certificate or some other small token of recognition.

Finally, make sure you can quantify your success by establishing metrics to measure usage and/or user satisfaction. Some systems have built-in features for tracking how often users visit or make updates to the site, but if you are not able to track usage that way, you can create a quick survey asking how often staff visits or updates, how satisfied they are with the system, and if they have any comments or suggestions. These statistics become particularly useful if you have similar statistics from whatever old system your library was using to compare them to, so you can highlight any increases in usage, communication, and interaction.

With proper planning and diligent follow through, any of the projects in this book are sure to be a practical and helpful resource for staff, and an asset to the library well into the future.

7

FUTURE TRENDS

This century has ushered in the rise of a collaboration culture, and with it the popularity of software that enables and supports connecting, sharing, interaction, and group effort. This comfort with creating and sharing digital content continues to make issues which involve the ownership, privacy, and security of that data extremely important. Going forward, it is likely that the following concepts will emerge or continue to grow in importance in the field of knowledge management and its related software systems:

- improved communication;
- facilitating connections;
- data portability;
- cross platform/device agnostic functionality; and
- security and privacy.

IMPROVED COMMUNICATION

It is almost universally accepted that e-mail has become a necessary evil for us, but that doesn't stop companies from continuing to try to improve upon it. As your inbox grows more out of control, you are less likely to notice and/or respond to important e-mails, which can lead to a breakdown in communication across an organization. Websites like Asana (https://asana.com/), Discourse (http://www.discourse.org/), Slack (https://slack.com/), and Trello (https://trello.com/) are aiming to change the way that people communicate at work and on the web. They focus on centering conversations around projects and priorities, maintaining the threaded structure of the conversation as it happens, and creating an easily accessible archive of past discussions. They also add in social features such as sharing and "liking" of posts, and they do a much better job of allowing users to add images and other embeddable content. Some of the products also allow you to add metadata to links and media, making searching, browsing, and linking to content easier. Because most of these services focus on teamwork, they can also include handy tools for things like checklists and deadlines.

FACILITATING CONNECTIONS

The basic concepts of knowledge management assert that knowledge is connected, and it is that connection that gives it value. In other words, knowledge is useless to an organization unless people can place it in context, and find ways to apply it to processes, services, and products. The goal of a good knowledge management system is to help connect people with information in a meaningful way. Sometimes people don't understand the topic enough to search or browse their way to the needed content. Sometimes, that content cannot be made implicit, and it's best to instead connect you with the person who understands the information and who can provide better answers than the system itself. Sometimes, the needed content is in *another*, separate system. With this in mind, knowledge management software must focus on finding ways to facilitate these connections. Rich metadata and protocols that allow systems to exchange information, or "talk to each other," allow users to connect with other users and connect with information across multiple systems.

Artificial intelligence technology can also keep track of the ways in which users interact with the software, and use that information to guide future interactions. For example, if users consistently access the same set of pages or articles in succession, the system can "guess" that the later pages are somehow related to the original search, even if they are not categorized as such. It can then present these pages as an option whenever someone new initiates a similar search. Systems can also track a user's behavior and make suggestions for content they might find useful, or alert them to such content if it becomes available in the future.

DATA PORTABILITY

Related to building systems that are able to exchange information, people are also paying more attention to whether or not they can get their data *out* of any given system. Software companies and web services fold shop, better deals become available, needs change, better *software* becomes available; these are the realities of today's information technology landscape. If your staff has put a lot of effort into adding and editing content in a knowledge base, you'd like to think there will be a way for you to extricate that content in such a way that it can easily be imported into another system.

In blogs and wikis, content can often be exported in standard formats such as XML or HTML, which can easily be imported into a different blog or wiki. Closed platforms, or "walled gardens" as they're often called, can make extracting content from the system difficult. For this reason, organizations may choose to implement open source software, in which the code is open for all to view. Keep in mind, however, that just because you have access to the software's code doesn't mean that you can always easily export content from the system. Most modern content management software stores content not in the system code itself, but in an attached database. Also keep in mind that if the system includes add-ons, widgets, or plug-ins, some of the content may not be in the main database(s), but stored within those applications instead.

CROSS PLATFORM/DEVICE AGNOSTIC FUNCTIONALITY

It's fairly common for users to be doing work across a variety of platforms and devices, like desktop computers, laptops, tablets, and smartphones, so it makes sense that they would want their software to work on all of them. Users want to be able to move seamlessly from one device and/or operating system to another, and they want the same features to be available, but optimized for any screen size, orientation, or processing speed. For this reason, many knowledge management systems have moved from the desktop (i.e., software installed on your own computer) to the cloud (i.e., software that is accessible from any machine with an internet connection.)

Technology has also enabled web developers to build sites that detect and optimize for whatever device they are being viewed on or accessed from. This trend has led some to argue that web services will move away from having separate apps that you install on your smartphone or tablet, toward having one "responsive" site that works well no matter the device. However it's likely that this shift will not be possible until web browsers for mobile devices evolve to be more feature-rich and easy-to-use.

SECURITY AND PRIVACY

The convenience of moving applications to the cloud, where your own organization does not have to worry about server administration or software updates, must be weighed against concerns about privacy and the security of your data and your user's data. Additionally, while free software used to monetize itself by selling ad space, more and more companies are now deciding to mine your data and sell that information instead.

Libraries are particularly concerned with the privacy of their users, so it's important that any systems they use are configured to save a minimal amount of identifying information, or that they at least keep that information secure. These concerns have led to a burgeoning market for third-party apps that deal with data encryption, anonymizing users, and more permanent data deletion. It's also likely that there will be a rise in "pay for privacy" options available in popular software packages, where you can purchase enterprise or business editions of the software which include a more secure environment.

Libraries should thus continue to be aware of this aspect of free products and adjust their usage accordingly, or invest in enterprise versions of the software. As these features develop and grow in availability, librarians should seek out and invest in the knowledge management systems that make privacy and security of data a priority.

Knowledge management can greatly improve organizational effectiveness, avoid knowledge loss, and incite innovation. The software and projects outlined in this book will help you create dynamic systems to capture knowledge and subject expertise for use within and beyond your library. Whether you choose to build a document management system with Google Drive, launch a library intranet site using Microsoft SharePoint, or create an FAQ knowledge base with LibAnswers, you'll be helping to make the most of your staff's collective know-how, talent, and experience, and adding considerable value to your organization.

RECOMMENDED READING

ARTICLES AND CASE STUDIES

Bottazzo, Violetta. "Intranet: A Medium of Internal Communication and Training." *Information Services and Use* 25, no. 2 (2005): 77–85. Accessed December 2, 2014. http://iospress.metapress.com/content/2l6e465rjq99uqre.

Costello, Kristen, and Darcy Del Bosque. "For Better or Worse: Using Wikis and Blogs for Staff Communication in an Academic Library." *Journal of Web Librarianship* 4, nos. 2–3 (2010): 143–60. Accessed July 5, 2014. http://dx.doi.org/10.1080/19322909.2010.502877.

Dahl, David. "An Unexpected Ally: Using Microsoft's SharePoint to Create a Departmental Intranet." *Journal of Web Librarianship* 4, nos. 2–3 (2010): 207–24. Accessed June 25, 2014. http://dx.doi.org/10.1080/19322909.2010.503092.

Diffin, Jennifer, Fanuel Chirombo, Dennis Nangle, and Mark De Jong. "A Point to Share: Streamlining Access Services Workflow through Online Collaboration, Communication, and Storage with Microsoft SharePoint." *Journal of Web Librarianship* 4, nos. 2–3 (2010): 225–37. Accessed June 25, 2014. http://dx.doi.org/10.1080/19322909.2010.501278.

Dworak, Ellie, and Keven Jeffery. "Wiki to the Rescue: Creating a More Dynamic Intranet." *Library Hi Tech* 27, no. 3 (2009): 403–10.

Forcier, Eric, Dinesh Rathi, and Lisa M. Given. "Knowledge Management and Social Media: A Case Study of Two Public Libraries in Canada." *Journal of Information & Knowledge Management* 12, no. 04 (2013). Accessed August 13, 2014. http://dx.doi.org/10.1142/S0219649213500391.

Haupt, Jon. "From Zero to Wiki: Proposing and Implementing a Library Wiki." *Journal of Web Librarianship* 1, no. 1 (2007): 77–92. Accessed July 5, 2014. http://dx.doi.org/10.1300/J502v01n01_06.

Kammerer, Judith J. "Migrating a Hospital Library Web Site to SharePoint and Expanding Its Usefulness." *Journal of Hospital Librarianship* 9, no. 4 (2009): 408–18. Accessed June 25, 2014. http://dx.doi.org/10.1080/15323260903250437.

Kim, Bohyun. "Organizational and Social Factors in the Adoption of Intranet 2.0: A Case Study." *Journal of Web Librarianship* 4, nos. 2–3 (2010): 187–206. Accessed June 25, 2014. http://dx.doi.org/10.1080/19322909.2010.501276.

Luo, Lili. "Reference Librarians' Adoption of Cloud Computing Technologies: An Exploratory Study." *Internet Reference Services Quarterly* 17, nos. 3–4 (2012): 147–66. Accessed September 4, 2014. http://dx.doi.org/10.1080/10875301.2013.765824.

Mavodza, Judith, and Patrick Ngulube. "Exploring the Use of Knowledge Management Practices in an Academic Library in a Changing Information Environment." *South*

African Journal of Libraries and Information Science 77, no. 1 (2011): 15–25. Accessed September 4, 2014. http://dx.doi.org/10.7553/77-1-63.

Ravas, Tammy. "Not Just a Policies and Procedures Manual Anymore: The University of Houston Music Library Manual Wiki." *Notes* 65, no. 1 (2008): 38–52. Accessed September 4, 2014. http://www.jstor.org/stable/30163607.

Rodriguez, Julia. "Social Software in Academic Libraries for Internal Communication and Knowledge Management: A Comparison of Two Reference Blog Implementations." *Internet Reference Services Quarterly* 15, no. 2 (2010): 107–24. Accessed September 11, 2014. http://dx.doi.org/10.1080/10875301003788323.

Sood, Chanderkanta, and D. S. Chaubey. "Knowledge Management and Its Application in Library Sciences." *Indian Journal of Library & Information Science* 8, no. 1 (2014). Accessed May 17, 2014. http://euroasiapub.org/IJRESS/Oct2011/5.pdf.

Stevens, Christy R. "Reference Reviewed and Re-Envisioned: Revamping Librarian and Desk-Centric Services with LibStARs and LibAnswers." *The Journal of Academic Librarianship* 39, no. 2 (2013): 202–14. Accessed September 11, 2014. http://dx.doi.org/10.1016/j.acalib.2012.11.006.

Townley, Charles T. "Knowledge Management and Academic Libraries." *College & Research Libraries* 62, no. 1 (2001): 44–55. Accessed May 17, 2014. http://dx.doi.org/10.5860/crl.62.1.44.

Xiaofen Dong, Elaine. "Using Blogs for Knowledge Management in Libraries." *CALA Occasional Paper Series* 2 (2008). Accessed November 19, 2014. http://cala-web.org/files/ops/OPSNov08.pdf.

BOOKS

Cawood, Stephen. *How to Do Everything Microsoft SharePoint 2013*. New York: McGraw-Hill Education, 2013.

Dalkir, Kimiz. *Knowledge Management in Theory and Practice*. Cambridge, MA: MIT Press, 2011.

Desouza, Kevin C., and Scott Paquette. *Knowledge Management: An Introduction*. New York: Neal-Schuman Publishers, 2011.

Dobbs, Aaron W. *Using LibGuides to Enhance Library Services*. Chicago, IL: ALA Techsource, 2013.

Frappaolo, Carl. *Knowledge Management*. Oxford: Capstone Publishing Ltd., 2006.

Harvard Business Review on Knowledge Management. Boston, MA: Harvard Business School, 1998.

Hobohm, Hans, ed. *Knowledge Management Libraries and Librarians Taking Up the Challenge*. Berlin: De Gruyter, 2004.

Kostagiolas, Petros. *Managing Intellectual Capital in Libraries beyond the Balance Sheet*. Oxford: Chandos Publishing, 2012.

Laplante, Phillip A. *Requirements Engineering for Software and Systems*. Boca Raton, FL: CRC Press, 2009.

Leary, Stephanie. *Wordpress for Web Developers: An Introduction for Web Professionals*. New York: Apress, 2013.

Lomas, Elizabeth. *Information Management Solutions: Communications and Collaboration in a Web 2.0 World*. London: Facet, 2010.

Londer, Olga, and Penelope Coventry. *Microsoft SharePoint 2013 Step by Step*. Redmond, Wash.: Microsoft Press, 2013.

McHale, Nina. *Designing and Developing Library Intranets*. London: Routledge, 2013.

Moore, Alannah. *Create Your Own Website Using WordPress in a Weekend*. New York: Focal Press, 2013.

Olinik, Mick, and Raena Jackson Armitage. *The WordPress Anthology*. Collingwood, Victoria, Australia: SitePoint, 2011.

ONLINE DOCUMENTATION AND HELP GUIDES

Commons In A Box: Documentation. Accessed December 3, 2014. http://commonsinabox.
    org/documentation.
"Discover SharePoint." Microsoft Download Center. Accessed December 3, 2014. http://
    www.microsoft.com/download/details.aspx?id=39372.
Google Drive Help Center. Accessed December 3, 2014. https://support.google.com/drive/.
"Installing WordPress." WordPress Codex. Accessed December 3, 2014. http://codex.
    wordpress.org/Installing_WordPress.
Microsoft TechNet: SharePoint Documentation. November 5, 2014. http://technet.
    microsoft.com/library/fp179725.aspx.
PBworks Educational Edition: Edumanual. Accessed December 3, 2014. http://edumanual.
    pbworks.com/w/page/58006589/Home.
Springshare Documentation and Support. Accessed December 19, 2014. http://support.
    springshare.com.
Springshare Help & Documentation: LibAnswers Help. Accessed December 3, 2014. http://
    help.springshare.com/libanswers.
Yammer Customer Success Center. Accessed December 3, 2014. https://about.yammer.com/
    success/.

INDEX

ABOUT THE AUTHOR

Valerie Forrestal is assistant professor at the City University of New York and serves as the web services librarian for the College of Staten Island. She has worked in academic libraries for over ten years, always in technology-based roles. She holds a MLIS, a MS in service oriented computing, and a MA in media arts. Forrestal has published and presented extensively on innovation and strategic collaboration in libraries and higher education, primarily focusing on UX-based web design and development, digital communications, and technology planning.

Forrestal stays active in her professional community as a mentor, as well as a conference and journal peer reviewer. She is also a *Choice* reviewer for STEM-related subject areas. Forrestal lives in the New York metro area with an embarrassing number of cats, cardigans, and tiaras. You can find her online at vforrestal.info or on Twitter as @vforrestal.